Misregulating Television

Stanley M. Besen
Thomas G. Krattenmaker
A. Richard Metzger, Jr.
John R. Woodbury

Misregulating

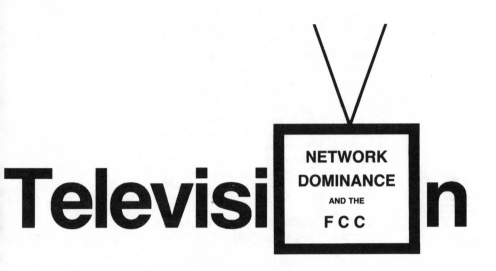

Televisi NETWORK DOMINANCE AND THE F C C n

NETWORK
DOMINANCE
AND THE
F C C

The University of Chicago Press
Chicago and London

Stanley M. Besen is a senior economist at the
Rand Corporation and was formerly codirector of
the FCC Network Inquiry. Also a former Inquiry
codirector, **Thomas G. Krattenmaker** is
professor of law at Georgetown University.
A. Richard Metzger, Jr., now a member of the
firm of Wald, Harkrader, and Ross in Washington,
D.C., was principal counsel to the Network
Inquiry, and **John R. Woodbury**, now vice
president of research and policy analysis for the
National Cable Television Association, was the
Inquiry's senior staff economist.

The University of Chicago Press, Chicago 60637
The University of Chicago Press, Ltd., London

93 92 91 90 89 88 87 86 85 84   54321

Library of Congress Cataloging in Publication Data
Main entry under title:

Misregulating television.

   Bibliography: p.
   Includes index.
   1. Television—Law and legislation—United States.
2. Television—Government policy—United States.
3. Television broadcasting—United States. 4. United
States. Federal Communications Commission. I. Besen,
Stanley M.
KF2840.M58   1984   343.73′09946   84-8738
ISBN 0-226-04415-7   347.3039946   347.3039946

Contents

v

Acknowledgments

Four people wrote this book but many more contributed to it. In particular, we benefited greatly from discussions with our colleagues on the FCC's Network Inquiry Special Staff. These included Michael Cummins, Gary Fournier, Terry Freundlich, Paul Jones, Mary Catherine Kilday, Bruce Levine, Donald Martin, Robert Mazer, and Sue Preskill. In addition, Dianne Beverly, Deborah Blue, and Donna Stewart provided invaluable staff support. We also received extensive research assistance from David Barsky, Sandra Edelman, Sean Flannery, and Barbara Gallagher.

This group of people, from whom we learned so much, was drawn together by the efforts of Charles Ferris, then chairman of the FCC; Frank Lloyd, assistant to the chairman; and Bob Bruce, the Commission's general counsel. They and their staffs spent many hours helping us. In this regard, we are also indebted to Greg Ballard, Dan Brenner, Dave Saylor, and Frank Washington. Many other FCC staff members also gave freely of their time and provided valuable advice. In this case it would be unfair not to single out Phil Verveer, the unofficial patron saint of the Network Inquiry, for his truly Herculean efforts to keep us on a sensible path.

We have also received extensive and valuable criticisms from many distinguished scholars in this field. Of these, we owe particular debts to Don Agostino, Michael Botein, Yale Braunstein, Bob Crandall, Dennis Dort, Douglas Ginsburg, Kristin Glen, Ken Jones, Roger Noll, Bruce Owen, Scot Powe, David Rice, Steve Salop, Tom Schuessler, and Ron Soligo.

People engaged in all facets of the television industry spent many hours supplying the information that undergirds this book. They are too numerous to list here, but had they not been so ready to provide information and submit to interviews, this project would still be in the research stage.

Although we owe much to all these people, they did not write the book and cannot be considered as subscribers to our conclusions. Indeed, we expect that many will wish to be heard in dissent.

The initial research underlying this book was undertaken during the FCC's Network Inquiry, but much of the research and all of the writing took place after the Inquiry concluded. These latter efforts were greatly facilitated by a succession of Georgetown University Law Center deans, David McCarthy and Robert Pitofsky, by writers' grants from the University, and by Anne Collins' faculty support services, which prepared the manuscript.

To all these kind and helpful people we express our deepest gratitude.

S.M.B.
T.G.K.
A.R.M.
J.R.W.

1   Introduction: Economic Regulation of Commercial Television Networks

The Federal Communications Commission, virtually from its inception in 1934, has been bedeviled by the issue of network dominance. This issue is frequently expressed as a concern that a few—usually three—corporations dictate the terms on which the business of broadcast home entertainment is conducted and reap the lion's share of profits from the broadcasting industry. During much of the first decade of the FCC's existence, the specific fear was that two firms operating three radio networks had monopolized the business of networking and dominated the programming selections of Commission licensees.[1] In the 1950s, as television became the more popular and profitable medium, the Commission noted with dread the emergence of three dominant television networks: ABC, CBS, and NBC. Consequently, between 1955 and 1970, the FCC conducted an almost uninterrupted series of studies of the phenomenon of television network dominance.[2] At the end of this period, the Code of Federal Regulations contained at least a dozen FCC rules limiting the business dealings between the commercial television networks and their affiliated broadcast stations and program suppliers.[3]

Although the Commission has promulgated no further rules proscribing television network conduct in the past ten years, such inactivity merely created a vacuum which the Department of Justice's Antitrust Division promptly filled. In 1972 the Department filed three substantively identical complaints against ABC, CBS, and NBC, charging that each of these firms had monopolized the business of exhibiting prime-time television entertainment programs. None of these cases ever went to trial; by 1981, however, each had been settled by entry of a consent decree that substantially circumscribes many of the terms on which ABC, CBS, and NBC may purchase programming.[4]

Despite three decades of relentless federal scrutiny, ABC, CBS, and NBC still "dominate" television, notwithstanding the Federal Communications Commission's view, held for over forty years, that such dominance can and should be restrained by limiting or dictating the networks' commercial practices. Accordingly, in 1977 the FCC announced yet another "network inquiry," directing the Commission's staff to inquire into the desirability and feasibility of adopting even more rules regulating network conduct, many of which had been suggested by the Justice Department's antitrust proceedings.[5]

We were among the group of economists and lawyers selected to head and staff the most recent FCC network inquiry. In October, 1980, we transmitted to the Commission the reports of our investigation. The admittedly immodest goal of the present study is not to repeat the various, detailed analyses of specific rules or proposed rules contained in our earlier reports, but rather to explore comprehensively the premises that consistently underlie the federal government's regulatory approach to television networks during the past three decades—that network dominance threatens important public policy goals and that such dominance may usefully be tempered or prevented by regulating the networks' commercial practices.

Several reasons suggest that such an examination is warranted at this time. First, despite the spate of governmental and private studies of television network structure and behavior, not since 1957 has anyone examined in a comprehensive integrated fashion the entire panoply of network relationships with advertisers, stations, and program suppliers. Second, in our former roles as investigators for the FCC, we were able to collect from a variety of industry sources large amounts of information not previously available to researchers. Consequently, we were able to test empirically a number of assertions concerning television industry behavior and the effect of FCC rules on that behavior to an extent not previously possible. Third, and most importantly, until quite recently television networks have been organized around a single technological and economic base in which a small number of local television stations, financed solely by payments from advertisers, were practically the exclusive source of televised home entertainment. For this reason, existing FCC rules proscribe only the behavior of networks that serve such conventional broadcasters. Today, however, more than 35 percent of television households in the United States subscribe to cable television systems; programming supported by direct viewer payments is widely offered via cable, microwave, videocassettes, videodiscs, and local television stations; and the FCC has proposed to authorize myriad additional outlets, employing existing and yet untested technology, to deliver programs to the home.[6] Whether existing or proposed regulations of conventional networks remain sound in this wider, more diverse broadcasting industry will soon become the central issue of television network economic regulation. This issue already arose in the 1970s with respect to radio networks; when the Commission examined its complex radio network regulations in light of modern developments, it determined to repeal most of those rules.[7]

Simply put, our goal is to employ the tools of legal and economic analysis to consider what functions the commercial practices of television networks serve, whether those practices undermine the goals of the Communications Act or national antitrust policy, and how regulation of these practices might affect the industry's performance in an expanded marketplace. Because our scope is broad, our resulting analysis is quite lengthy. Our approach, however, is straightforward. First, we define the economic functions of television networks, describe the extent to which these entities do in fact dominate the television industry, and explain many of the factors that cause this dominance (chapter 2). We then develop a series of criteria by which to measure the theoretical desirability and practical utility of regulations of the commercial practices and economic structure of television networks (chapter 3). To complete the necessary background, we survey the history and present system of federal economic regulation of television network practices and organization and describe those proposals for additional regulations that have been studied most seriously in the past decade (chapter 4).

Our assessment of the role of regulation is divided into three distinct types of controls: those regulating the network-affiliate dealings (chapter 5 and 6), those governing agreements between networks and program suppliers (chapter 7 and 8), and those limiting the types of entities networks may own or control (chapter 9). The evaluations of rules regulating contract terms are preceded by extensive analyses of the economic conditions that give rise to these terms. We thus attempt to describe the practical effects of existing and proposed regulations so that these effects may be measured against the criteria derived earlier. In all cases we seek to evaluate regulations in the contexts of both the television industry for which these rules were devised and that industry as it is evolving. Finally, we seek to describe a regulatory pattern that is well-suited to the modern television industry and to identify the underlying causes of previous failures in policy analysis (chapter 10).

2   Network Dominance

Measures of Network Dominance

Although the phrase "network dominance" is sufficiently elastic to encompass a wide variety of specific meanings, by any definition it exists. ABC, CBS, and NBC do indeed "dominate" the television broadcasting industry and form funnels through which most of our television programs flow. For the month of December, 1983, ABC, CBS, and NBC captured 80 percent of the prime-time television viewing audience.[1] In calendar year 1980 these firms, along with network-owned stations and affiliated stations, accounted for about 90 percent of both the revenues and profits of the television broadcasting industry.[2]

Independent commercial television stations (i.e., those not affiliated with ABC, CBS, or NBC) do exist, but these stations are not independent by choice; they broadcast exclusively in markets already served by affiliates of each network. Despite diligent searches, we have been unable to locate a single instance in the past twenty-five years when any commercial television station rejected an ABC, CBS, or NBC affiliation offer in order to remain independent or to affiliate with a fourth network.[3] Similarly, firms that produce programs for television regard ABC, CBS, and NBC as a separate market; with few exceptions, they do not at present believe that programs of the sort that the dominant networks acquire can be produced for and sold station-by-station in the syndication market or developed for networks composed of cable television systems or other local outlets employing new technologies, although this is likely to change as cable penetration increases.[4] No firm other than ABC, CBS, or NBC can presently offer an advertiser the opportunity, in one transaction, to gain commercial positions

4

in every part of the broadcast day and on every day in the broadcast week in programs offered to virtually all U.S. television households.

The preceding data do no more than illustrate what is common knowledge—that three firms exercise enormous power in the television industry and receive large profits from that business. To understand more fully the sources of network dominance, however, requires more detailed analysis. Three questions are central. Why are networks important to the industry? Why do networks of the size and configuration of ABC, CBS, and NBC arise and outperform most others? Why are there only three such firms? Elementary physical and economic aspects of broadcasting go far to answer the first two questions. The third raises difficult questions concerning the interpretation of government, industry, and network behavior.

Why Networks are Dominant

Television networks arise because of the interplay of physics and economics. The physical properties of broadcast television signals limit their range; consequently, no single terrestrial television transmitter can reach as much as 10 percent of the U.S. populace today. To provide television service to the entire nation via broadcast stations that utilize the airwaves, then, television signal transmitters (television stations) must be placed throughout the country. That is, the laws of physics dictate that if over-the-air television service is to be earthbound, it must also be provided locally or regionally.

Economic principles, however, pull in the opposite direction. A television program is what economists term a "public good"; its broadcast to one viewer does not reduce its availability or utility to other viewers.[5] A program produced for and transmitted in New York can be broadcast also in Los Angeles at no additional expense aside from the costs of getting the program across the country and operating an additional transmitting tower.

In a nutshell, then, what networks do is to offer physically separated local television stations the economies of scale associated with television program production. By supplying identical programs to many stations, networks both increase the financial base available to fund program production, enabling more expensive programs to be produced, and reduce the per-viewer costs of producing and distributing any given program.

These elementary and unalterable principles explain why nationally distributed television programming will usually have greater viewer appeal than programs produced and aired only locally. The former can cater more lavishly to viewer tastes, yet at a lower cost per viewer than the latter. Nationally distributed programs will not always win out, of course. Viewer tastes may vary from place to place; hence the prevalence of locally produced television news programs. The producer of a program may derive other revenues from producing it, so that large amounts can be spent on production even if exhibition rights are not sold on a national basis. For example, both the existence of gate receipts and variations in tastes among localities probably explain why many professional sports events are telecast regionally or locally rather than nationally.

Economics of Full-scale Networking

Such exceptions limit, but do not undermine, the principle that nationally disseminated programming will usually be more valuable to viewers, advertisers, and stations than local shows. This principle, however, explains only why national programs are prevalent; it does not explain why every mass-distributed program or program series is not distributed by a separate network. ABC, CBS, and NBC are dominant not because they are successful networks, but because they successfully operate full-scale networks, offering programs every day of the week throughout most of the broadcast day.

At least a partial answer to this question is that the economies yielded by networking are not exhausted in the provision of a single program. First, the existence of a full-scale network permits advertisers, in a single transaction, to purchase time on many stations and within diverse programs, and assures them that each ad will appear at the same time in each market. Such a purchasing scheme is obviously less costly than negotiating contracts with each station individually and also makes it easier for the advertiser to predict the audience it will reach. Second, full-scale operation permits the network and a station to negotiate a single contract that covers the processes of offer and acceptance, as well as the amount and manner of compensation for many programs, thus holding program acquisition and distribution costs below what they would be if networks offered service on a program-by-program and station-by-station basis. Third, a network that provides a schedule of programs can spread the risk of program failure and thus predict more accurately its rate of success than can a network offering only a single program. Because at present the networks finance a substantial portion of the cost of program development, spreading the risk across a large number of programs is a considerable advantage.

The foregoing is not an exhaustive description of the economies that result from full-scale networking, but probably explains why networks that offer few programs are unlikely to provide substantial competition to the dominant networks. Of course, the economies of full-scale networking are not limitless. Indeed, no network offers programs every hour of every day. Variations in local tastes, limits on the amount national advertisers wish to spend on network television, FCC rules on network-affiliate agreements, and bargaining between networks and their affiliated stations over the distribution of profits from broadcasting are some of the factors that work to limit the length of network schedules. Whether networks nevertheless grow beyond the size dictated by the economies they generate is the question we address next.

Size vs. Fewness: The Central Issue

In sum, fundamental and unavoidable physical phenomena and economic conditions virtually dictate two principles respecting network organization and behavior. First, networks, defined as firms that distribute programs nationally or regionally, will necessarily dominate any industry providing home television entertainment programs because programs produced for mass distribution typically will be more advantageous, to industry members and to viewers, than locally produced shows. Second, full-scale networks, defined as those like ABC, CBS, and NBC that offer many programs on many or all broadcast days in most or all time slots, enjoy economies of scale that give them a competitive edge in most instances over networks that offer substantially more limited fare. Neither of these principles is limitless. Nonnetwork programs do prove profitable in many cases. Smaller networks frequently offer programs that outperform network fare. The fact, however, that these principles are limited should not obscure their general validity or importance. The inescapable conclusion is that firms offering an extensive network schedule enjoy substantial competitive advantages in the broadcast industry as currently financed and structured.

For these reasons, governmental regulation of network organization and behavior would be senseless if such regulation were intended simply to prohibit networking or full-scale networks. At best, regulation of that aspect of network dominance can produce only equivalent programming at higher costs. Indeed, the FCC recognized this principle in its initial comprehensive examination of the role of networks in the 1930s radio industry and has not questioned that conclusion subsequently.[6] The question, therefore, that must be addressed in considering the appropriate method of regulating network commercial practices is not why networks are important to the broadcast industry, or why full-scale networks enjoy such competitive success, but rather why the number of effective competing networks is so low. The question whether existing networks are "too large" is thus necessarily subsidiary to the question how many networks exist. Put another way, when the industry's basic technological and economic conditions are understood, the concerns that should emerge from statistics describing network dominance are fears of fewness, not of size per se. To understand why so few networks exist, one must examine the barriers to entry that potential networks confront.

Why So Few Networks Exist

It is not true, strictly speaking, that there are only three television networks. Several other networks, such as Home Box Office and Showtime, interconnect cable systems and offer identical programming simultaneously to viewers across the United States. Independent, conventional television stations occasionally band together to finance programs to be shown on stations from coast to coast. When a successful network prime-time entertainment series completes its network run, the series is usually sold to many stations around the country for rebroadcast.

It is not correct, furthermore, that, from the inception of television broadcasting, there have always been three conventional, full-scale networks. The NBC television network was established before CBS became a significant force, both were substantially more powerful than ABC in television's early stages, and the DuMont network coexisted with ABC, CBS, and NBC in the early 1950s.

Nevertheless, it is true that no television network exists, or has existed since at least 1957, that approaches ABC, CBS, and NBC in income, profits, length of schedule, or numbers of viewers reached. Logically, the industry may be limited to three full-scale networks for either of two reasons. First, marketplace conditions may be such that a fourth full-scale network would not be profitable, even if that fourth firm encountered no entry barriers. If this is not the case, then some important barriers to entry must exist. The latter proposition is, we think, firmly supported by the available evidence.

Levels of Viewer and Advertiser Demand

First, recent economic studies convincingly confirm the hypothesis that, in the absence of entry barriers, a fourth network would be profitable.[7] The most dramatic conclusion of these studies is that, if all networks competed on an equal footing with respect to the number and quality of local outlets, at least one and possibly as many as three additional advertiser-supported full-scale networks could operate profitably, even if total industry advertising revenues remained constant while increased competition among networks caused program costs to rise.

Second, developing industry structure appears to confirm the conclusions of these economic studies. For example, as cable penetration has increased, a number of networks have arisen to serve local cable systems. About twenty advertiser-supported cable networks now exist.[8] Unless every one of these entrepreneurs has exaggerated its likelihood of success, at least some of these new cable networks should be expected to survive as full-scale operations were cable to become as widely available as conventional broadcasting. Indeed, since viewer fees may be an additional source of support, cable penetration probably need not equal that of conventional broadcasting in order for cable networks to compete effectively.

Barriers to Entry Imposed by Government Regulation

If additional networks could be operated profitably, why do they not exist? One possibility is that the existing dominant networks, individually or collectively, have engaged in practices that preclude or inhibit the development of potential new networks. Whether this is true is, of course, a central problem one must confront in evaluating governmental regulation of networks. As we demonstrate below, however, it is frequently quite difficult to determine whether a particular network practice has an exclusionary purpose or effect, or is rather an economically efficient response to existing competitive conditions.

For these reasons, it is important at the outset to emphasize that, whatever judgment is eventually made concerning the effects of network practices, overwhelming evidence proves that a series of FCC policies effectively blockaded new network entry at least until the mid-1970s, after which many of these policies were abandoned or were circumvented by technological developments. Three types of Commission policies have especially disadvantaged potential networks and are discussed below in ascending order of importance.

1. *Interconnection Costs and FCC Policy*

As noted above, one cost of networking is the expense of interconnecting stations. Prior to the advent of satellites capable of transmitting television signals, the only method for interconnecting stations, short of making multiple copies of films or tapes of programs and distributing them through the mail, was to employ a terrestrial relay system. In the early stages of television industry growth, the FCC permitted AT&T a virtual monopoly over providing this service and, to the present day, AT&T charges substantially different rates for "full-time" and "part-time" service. Whether this discrepancy in rates is justified by differences in the cost of providing the two types of services has been hotly disputed.[9] Clearly, however, the discrepancy has affected the conditions of entry confronting potential networks, and the FCC has only recently been able or willing to take steps to ameliorate this handicap.

Only ABC, CBS, and NBC offer program schedules as extensive as AT&T's full-time service. To illustrate the effects on network costs imposed by the difference in interconnection rates, the Network Inquiry staff calculated charges in 1980 for two hypothetical networks, each requiring 4,585 miles of microwave relay to interconnect ten stations. A network paying full-time rates would pay $9,239 per day for interconnection; a part-time network transmitting a single one-hour program would pay $9,239 for that one hour.[10] This single illustration dramatically reveals the differences in per-program terrestrial interconnection costs confronting part-time and full-time networks. One effect, of course, is to impose a severe cost disadvantage on any fledgling network, thereby increasing the scale on which entry must be attempted.

In the past decade the FCC has taken steps that reduce the interconnection disadvantage confronting new networks. With respect to terrestrial systems, the Commission has permitted firms to operate private systems that bypass the AT&T monopoly,[11] and allowed intermediaries to purchase blocks of time and to resell that time to part-time users.[12] These actions should go far to ensure that AT&T cannot charge differential rates that are not cost-justified.[13] The FCC also has proposed to replace the present AT&T full-time/part-time rate structure with a two-part tariff that could substantially reduce the differential between full-time and part-time charges.[14]

More dramatic changes have occurred because of the introduction of communications satellites. The FCC has permitted relatively open entry into the business of owning broadcast satellites,[15] and unrestricted entry into the business of reselling satellite interconection time.[16] Further, in 1977 the Commission repealed its earlier rules establishing technical design requirements for devices (known as "earth stations") that receive satellite television transmissions and requiring that earth stations be licensed by the Commission.[17] Earth stations now cost as little as $4,000 and the hypothetical one-hour network described above could interconnect via satellite the same ten broadcast outlets (if all have earth stations) for a few hundred dollars.[18]

2. *FCC Restrictions on Program Services*

The second manner in which the Commission has impeded new network entry is by limiting the kinds of services nonconventional networks may offer to the public. Until recently, the FCC substantially restricted both distant signal importation by cable television and the programs that could be offered, via broadcast or otherwise, in return for direct viewer payments.

Cable system signal importation. Between 1962 and 1980 the Commission enforced a variety of rules, all of which had two common consequences: cable systems, especially in large cities, were severely limited in the number of distant signals (i.e., broadcast stations outside the geographic market served by the cable system) they could import and (until 1976) cable systems were limited in the geographic areas from which they could import signals.[19] By conscious design, these rules had the twin effect of retarding the growth of cable television and of precluding the option of establishing a substantial network by interconnecting one (or a few) conventional broadcast stations and several cable systems.

As these Commission rules were first relaxed and then repealed,[20] cable television penetration leaped forward and independent broadcast stations whose signals are distributed across the country (so-called superstations) blossomed. For example, WTBS-TV of Atlanta was imported in March, 1984 by 6,075 cable systems with 29 million subscribers.[21]

Pay programming. For an extended period, the Commission also set out to prevent the dissemination of television entertainment programs paid for directly by viewers. Conventional television stations can, by broadcasting a scrambled signal, charge viewers for decoding it. In industry parlance, such broadcasting is designated as subscription television (STV). The FCC refused to authorize any subscription television, except on an experimental basis, until 1968. At that time, the Commission authorized subscription television generally, but simultaneously, in a rerun of its cable TV performance, committed infanticide by regulation. Among the restrictions placed on pay TV were those banning entirely the broadcast for pay of series programming, commercials, virtually all major sports events, and, with minor exceptions, any theatrical feature film that had been released more than two years before its STV broadcast.[22] In 1970 these "antisiphoning" rules were extended to cable television, which was then the only other available medium for delivering pay television to homes.[23] Only minor modifications were made in these STV and pay cable rules until 1977, when the D.C. Circuit struck down all of the cable pay TV rules.[24] A year later, the Commission removed its antisiphoning rules for pay programs offered by over-the-air stations.[25]

No easy method exists for assessing the extent to which the FCC's antisiphoning rules imposed barriers to potential networks. As illustrated in the next section, these rules were accompanied by other regulations, based on the Commission's spectrum management authority, that until 1980 lessened the attractiveness to viewers of cable service and until 1982 substantially confined the number of STV stations and the markets in which they could be operated. Consequently, the full extent of viewer demand for pay television service has yet to be determined.

Nevertheless, all available evidence since the deletion of these rules indicates that the antisiphoning restrictions did in fact deter network growth. For example, in early 1976, 650,000 households subscribed to pay cable; by the end of 1983 that figure had increased to 17.9 million. In 1977, the two largest full-service pay cable networks, Home Box Office and Showtime, had 700,000 and 61,000 subscribers respectively; in March, 1984 they had 13.5 million and 5 million.[26] Demand for STV could not be manifest in new offerings as rapidly because of FCC limitations. The first modern STV station came on the air in 1977. By the end of 1983, twenty more stations were operating, twenty-eight others had been authorized by the Commission, and additional applications were pending for thirty-seven channels in twenty-one cities.[27] These data strongly suggest that the FCC's earlier pay program policies, which confined commercial television to an exclusively advertiser-supported system and thereby limited the financial base upon which additional networks might be erected, substantially hindered potential new networks.

3. FCC Spectrum Management Policies

The third and most important set of these Commission policies that have acted as a barrier to formation of additional networks has sprung directly or indirectly from the FCC's spectrum management responsibilities. Collectively, these policies made a fourth, full-scale over-the-air network inconceivable until very recently.

The FCC's basic charter, the Communications Act of 1934, gives the Commission two principal responsibilities concerning access to the electromagnetic spectrum that materially affect the number of networks and the extent of competition among them. First, the Commission is empowered to allocate the spectrum among different uses, to determine, for example, which part of the spectrum will be used for FM radio broadcasting. Second, the Commission then assigns spectrum space to specific geographic areas, deciding, for example, whether a transmitter broadcasting on a certain portion of the allocated AM radio spectrum may be based in Newark, N.J., or in New York City. In addition to these express powers, the Supreme Court has agreed with the FCC that the Commission also enjoys "ancillary jurisdiction" over cable television transmission, at least to the extent necessary to protect its allocation and assignment policies.[28]

As noted above, television networks exist because of the economies that accrue from interconnecting geographically dispersed local television stations. Consequently, no action by the FCC could have a greater effect on the conditions of entry confronting television networks than its allocation and assignment decisions since these decisions affect both the number and location of broadcast stations. If, for example, the Commission had exercised its panoply of powers so as to limit every U.S. household to receiving just one television signal, then one full-scale broadcast network, at most, could have emerged.

What the Commission has actually done is somewhat more complicated, although only slightly less draconian. In brief, the FCC initially exercised its spectrum allocation and assignment of powers in a manner that almost guaranteed that no more than three full-scale, advertiser-supported nationwide networks that employed conventional broadcast stations as local outlets would arise. Subsequently, the Commission utilized the same powers, as well as its ancillary jurisdiction over cable, to retard the growth of new technologies or pay TV systems that might have provided alternative bases on which to establish rival networks.

Barriers confronting potential traditional networks. That the Commission's spectrum management policies blocked entry into conventional, advertiser-supported, over-the-air networking is now accepted as commonplace among scholars, although this fact probably was not fully understood at the time the Commission's key decisions were made. Recently, Thomas Schuessler exhaustively summarized the number and variety of restrictive steps the FCC has taken in this area, so that a simple summary should suffice here.[29]

Three distinct FCC spectrum management decisions embodied in a 1952 order have limited the number of conventional networks.[30] First, the Commission chose to assign only limited portions of the VHF and UHF bands to television transmission. If more bandwidth had been given to television, then more stations could have existed and perhaps provided a base for additional networks. Second, to utilize the spectrum assigned to television, the Commission determined to assign, wherever possible, at least one television broadcast station to each U.S. community. In most areas of the United States distinct communities are frequently in close proximity. To avoid interference among signals, the FCC must limit the area television stations serve. But, to authorize transmitters in small communities, the Commission had to limit the number of stations assigned to larger cities. The effect was to limit the number of networks that might arise by restricting the number of available outlets that networks might use to reach large numbers of viewers. Third, in most cases the Commission determined to place both VHF and UHF stations in the same market ("intermixture," in industry parlance). UHF television signals have always been technically inferior to VHF and will remain so for at least the foreseeable future. For this reason, UHF stations compete under a great handicap with their VHF counterparts. Intermixture has affected the number of stations available for network affiliation because UHF stations often cannot survive in intermixed markets. The same policy also affects the nature of competition among those networks that do arise, because a network with a high percentage of UHF affiliates is handicapped in competing vigorously with a network employing primarily VHF outlets.

The interaction of the Commission's choices to limit the TV band, assign stations locally, and intermix VHF and UHF stations produced an overall national assignment plan for commercial television stations, adopted in 1952, that virtually guaranteed that no more than three full-scale, nationwide commercial networks could arise to serve conventional, over-the-air, advertiser-supported stations. The plan does not provide equally valuable outlets in enough markets to enable a fourth network to achieve sufficient economies of scale to enable it to compete on equal, or reasonably close, terms with the other three. This effect can be portrayed most easily by comparing the national coverage the dominant networks obtain with that available to potential new entrants. In 1979, stations owned by or affiliated with ABC, CBS, and NBC reached 98.1, 96.5 and 96.9 percent of U.S.

television households respectively. About 13 percent of those households receiving ABC obtained ABC programming via UHF; for CBS and NBC, the figures were 7 percent and 10 percent respectively.[31]

The FCC's table of assignments would impose a dual handicap on any potential additional network. First, such additional networks would face a coverage handicap. If all assigned commercial television frequencies were on the air, a fourth network could reach at most 91.3 percent of U.S. TV households; a fifth could reach 81.1 percent and a sixth 66.8 percent.[32] Second, potential additional networks would face a UHF handicap because, in many markets, the newcomer's UHF affiliate would have to compete with three VHF affiliates of the incumbent networks. Again assuming that all assigned stations were operational, a fourth network could offer only 36 percent of TV households signals technically comparable to those of all three existing networks, and 41 percent of all TV households would receive a fourth network from a UHF affiliate while obtaining ABC, CBS, and NBC programs from a VHF station.[33]

Of course, additional networks are more likely to be erected on the base of operational, rather than assigned, stations. Many stations that have been assigned are not in operation, principally because of the Commission's local assignment and intermixture policies. That is, many stations were authorized in markets too small to support them and other assignments have never been utilized because they authorize UHF stations in markets where many VHF stations also exist. Assuming that a potential new network does not bid away affiliates of the dominant three, the existing base of commercial stations available to such a network would impose severe coverage and UHF handicaps on it. Using existing stations, a fourth network in 1980 could reach at most 63.6 percent of U.S. TV households; a fifth could serve 40.8 percent and a sixth 27.8 percent. Moreover, the fourth network, completely shut out of 36 percent of all households, could also reach another 26 percent with the only UHF affiliate in the market.[34]

The preceding statistics compel three conclusions concerning the effects of FCC spectrum management policies on the prospects for new networks that interconnect conventional advertiser-supported television broadcast stations. First, it is almost unthinkable that, more than thirty years after the FCC adopted its spectrum assignment plan for television, a fifth conventional network could arise. Second, continued increases in advertiser demand for television time and further diminutions in the UHF handicap eventually might produce conditions under which the base for an almost-equivalent fourth network could exist; such conditions, however, clearly do not now exist and were no more than a pipe dream a decade ago. Finally, from the outset of television broadcasting to the present, no possibility, however remote, has existed that more than three networks of the sort represented by ABC, CBS, and NBC could operate profitably. Entry could occur only if a new network displaced one of the dominant three (for example, by bidding away affiliates or purchasing the network), an outcome that would still yield only three networks, or put together a combination of affiliates that included outlets other than conventional, advertiser-supported broadcast stations in some markets.

Barriers confronting potential networks offering pay programming. A variety of Commission policies precluded the option of putting together a combination of affiliates employing disparate technologies. Until very recently, a firm desiring to establish a full-scale network financed in whole or in part by direct viewer payments would have encountered insuperable barriers. As already noted, the Commission severely restricted pay cable program offerings until 1978 and for another year similarly limited over-the-air pay offerings. Moreover, until 1979 the FCC refused to permit more than one subscription TV station in any community,[35] and only recently repealed the so-called complement of four rule that prohibited a broadcast station from offering subscription TV unless at least four "free" (i.e., advertiser-supported) commercial stations broadcast in its community.[36] This rule effectively prohibited broadcast pay TV in all except eighty-eight U.S. communities, only forty-three of which have operating stations that are permitted to offer pay programming. Together with the mix of FCC policies restricting cable growth generally, these policies made inconceivable, at least until 1978, the establishment of a pay TV network sufficiently large to compete with full-scale conventional networks. Indeed, these FCC policies were adopted precisely to forestall such a development.

Barriers confronting potential networks employing unconventional technology. A firm desiring to establish a full-scale, nationwide, advertiser-supported network in the 1970s faced no better prospects than a fledgling pay TV network. As we have seen, sufficient conventional stations of comparable technical quality are not in operation nor have they been assigned. Until recently, the only other technology available for providing local affiliation outlets has been cable television. The Commission, however, stifled cable development (especially in larger markets) with its anti-siphoning rules until 1978, its distant signal importation limits, in effect until

1980, and a variety of other rules limiting the fare cable could offer. Consequently, no other technology was available to close the coverage handicap confronting an additional network. Again, this result was precisely what the Commission intended. The cornerstone of the FCC's argument that rules should be adopted to restrict cable growth was the proposition that cable should not be allowed to undermine the agency's plan governing the provision of over-the-air television.

Relaxation of Regulatory Barriers to Entry

Commercial television networking essentially began in 1948. Thirty years later, as a result of economic forces and FCC policies, it was virtually unthinkable that any network could compete vigorously with the dominant three full-scale, nationwide, advertiser-supported networks. Networks that operated on a less than full-scale, nationwide basis faced much higher interconnection costs and failed to realize the many economies of full-scale networking. To establish a full-scale nationwide network was next to impossible given the FCC's spectrum management, pay TV and cable distant-signal importation rules.

By the end of this decade, however, conditions are likely to be substantially different. We noted above that part-time networks no longer need pay distinctly higher interconnection rates, the Commission no longer limits cable systems' importation of distant signals, and the FCC's "antisiphoning" rules have now been repealed. All these actions have apparently had important and immediate effects in increasing the number of networks and there is reason to believe they will continue to do so.

Perhaps most importantly, the barriers to entry raised by the Commission's spectrum management decisions are rapidly being eroded. To be sure, the basic 1952 allocation plan remains firmly intact and no release of those constraints is under serious consideration. In recent years, however, the Commission proposed three intiatives which, if adopted, would ameliorate the restrictions on network entry imposed by the 1952 scheme.

First, the Commission in 1980 proposed to permit additional VHF station assignments to be "dropped in" to the existing table of assignments.[37] Taking advantage of technological developments since 1952, and operating at lower power than conventional stations, the drop-ins would avoid interference even though they operate at shorter distances from existing stations than were permitted previously. The Commission's Broadcast Bureau has calculated that, under these new technical standards, at least one VHF drop-in could be authorized in seventy-two of the top one hundred television markets. Thirty-five of these markets, containing 22.6 percent of U.S. television households, currently have only three VHF stations.

Second, in 1982, the FCC created a new broadcast service by adopting rules governing low-power television.[38] From the inception of commercial television, low-power television stations have been employed to pick up signals from conventional television stations and retransmit these signals at boosted strength on another channel, thereby extending the originating stations' reach. These "translators" originally came into use to serve remote areas. When authorized by the Commission, translators were permitted only to broadcast on UHF with very low-power transmitters and were forbidden to originate programming, sell advertising time, or broadcast on a pay TV basis. The 1982 rules eliminate all programming restrictions for low-power TV, permit the service to operate in both the VHF and UHF bands, and increase substantially the power at which these stations may operate.[39] All these changes were advocated specifically to create a nation-wide low-power service that might coexist with the conventional national television broadcast service. If the initial response to this proposal is any indication of its long-term appeal, that goal might well be realized; the Commission had about 32,000 applications pending for low-power stations in 1983.

Third, as noted earlier, the Commission in 1982 repealed the "complement of four" rule for over-the-air pay TV.[40] As long as that rule remained in effect, a subscription TV network affiliating with existing stations could reach no more than 41 percent of U.S. television households. Without the rule, even if the network affiliated only with existing stations not affiliated with ABC, CBS, or NBC, another 23 percent of TV households would potentially be available to it.

Outside the VHF and UHF band the potential exists for much more far-reaching changes to take place. Prerecorded videocassettes and video-discs, products of recent technological innovation, are being widely marketed. Although this distribution system does not involve the interconnection of local television outlets, it permits firms to realize many of the mass-distribution economies of networking. Satellites that broadcast television pictures directly to the home will be able to perform similar network functions. Direct broadcast satellites (DBS) are now undoubtedly technically feasible and in 1979 were authorized by the international body governing spectrum allocation. The Federal Communications Commission only adopted interim rules governing DBS authorizations in 1982,[41] so no one can describe with assurance when DBS will be fully authorized in the United States or how the system will be structured. The Commission's staff has concluded, however, that the DBS system eventually authorized will provide a capacity to supply to most U.S. homes a minimum of six to ten additional television channels. DBS uses extraordinarily high frequencies, so its introduction need not displace any other television broadcast systems. In 1982 the FCC granted construction permits to eight applicants, on the condition that they begin construction within one year.[42]

In addition, two technologies that are not so new have increased potential as a result of recent FCC decisions. Cable television is now almost entirely free of Commission regulation and functioning cable systems are now available to more than 66.5 percent of U.S. households. Multipoint distribution service (MDS) delivers television programming via microwave in yet another segment of the spectrum. MDS was authorized by the Commission in 1962, but did not become a popular service for delivering television entertainment until the post-1977 growth of pay TV. By June 1983, 103 MDS systems offered television programming. The Commission, however, had granted only two channels capable of television transmission to MDS in the fifty largest markets and one channel in all others, so that hundreds of applications for additional systems could not be processed rapidly because they made competing claims for the same spectrum space. In 1983 the FCC sought to break this logjam by allocating two additional groups of four MDS channels to every market and proposing the use of a lottery procedure to award the newly authorized channels.[43]

Cumulatively, the Commission's recent spectrum management actions and proposals—permitting the VHF drop-ins, establishing a low-power TV service, repealing limitations on STV stations, expanding MDS facilities, and withdrawing from cable regulation—if adopted and carried out as promised, when combined with the technological development of DBS, videocassettes, and videodiscs, will necessarily reduce substantially the coverage handicap confronting new networks by the end of this decade. Potential entrants, we have noted, have already been relieved of the burdens created by disadvantageous interconnection rates, limits on cable system distant signal importation, and antisiphoning rules. By employing one or a combination of these new technologies, with or without supplementation by conventional broadcast stations, firms wishing to establish full-scale, nationwide television entertainment networks should be able to reach increasingly large numbers of U.S. television households at the end of this decade.

The Relationship between Entry Barriers and Network
Conduct Regulations

The significance of these developments for an appropriate analysis of the
issue of "network dominance" cannot be overemphasized. The present
behavior of the dominant networks, and the FCC's rules regulating that
behavior, originated in a system where governmental policies virtually
precluded entry by additional networks. Because those entry barriers are
eroding, in the future these networks' conduct, and the Commission's
response to it, will be shaped in a substantially more competitive environment among networks.

3 Criteria for Evaluating Regulations of Television Network Structure and Behavior

To analyze an industry's commercial practices, one of course should first specify the criteria by which those practices may be evaluated. Nevertheless, our experience has been that the point deserves emphasis, however commonplace it may appear, because the television industry presents peculiar problems that make assessment of its performance particularly difficult.

Established Goals of Network Economic Regulation

Ideally, FCC regulation of commercial television network economic structure and behavior should be designed to achieve three goals. First, economic theory teaches that society is best off when economic units behave efficiently. Consequently, the Commission should establish regulations that promote efficiency and avoid those that penalize or proscribe it. Second, television today is the principal source of both entertainment and information for most Americans. Therefore, regulation should strive to channel the industry's performance so that it provides an environment in which all members of society receive the benefits associated with the enjoyment of First Amendment freedoms. Third, the Commission must ensure the accomplishment of the policies established in its charter, the Communications Act of 1934.

Sources of Difficulty in Measuring Achievement of Goals

The goals of enhancing efficiency, realizing First Amendment values, and promoting Communications Act policies appear to be widely agreed upon.

21

They are, however, abstract terms. For a number of reasons, none of these general goals can be translated easily into specific criteria by which to measure the industry's performance or the Commission's supervision of it.

The Problem of "Public Goods"

Because television programs are public goods,[1] the typical normative economic criterion of allocative efficiency cannot easily be applied to assess industry behavior. Were we to evaluate the conduct of the necktie industry, for example, we would expect to be able to assess that conduct by inquiring simply whether any consumer willing to pay the additional cost of producing a necktie is denied the opportunity to purchase one. If this condition were fulfilled, we could be sure that no one—producer or consumer—could be made better off without making someone else worse off.

Television program production and distribution cannot be analyzed so simply. Since no additional cost is incurred in serving at least some additional viewers, if programs are sold to viewers for a fee, exclusion of those potential viewers who would be willing to pay a positive price below the established price is inefficient.[2] If programs are financed by advertising revenue, with no explicit charge to viewers, however, the amount charged for the programs will reflect the number of people who watch, not the value they place on the program. Consequently, we cannot be sure that programs which viewers collectively value at more than their production costs will be produced. For example, ten thousand viewers may value "Gilligan's Island" at $1, while an equally costly alternative, "Weekly Boxing," is valued by one thousand viewers at $11. An advertiser-supported network will air "Gilligan's Island," even though its alternative is more highly valued.[3]

The Problem of Defining First Amendment Economic Goals

When we consider the social role of the television industry in providing a national forum for news and entertainment, the case for developing criteria solely from normative economic theory weakens further. Even if we could know with assurance that the economically efficient amount and types of television programs were being offered and that the resources used to produce them were efficiently allocated, we should still inquire further whether the industry's performance may be gauged by standards that take account of the fact that television is an important comunications medium.

Almost no body of analysis exists, however, that describes what these standards might be. When one reflects on the history of application of economic policy toward communications media, one can only conclude that there is no accepted, explicit set of standards by which to measure whether and how a communication medium's economic structure or behavior affects the realization of First Amendment values.

The Vagueness of the Communications Act

Finally, the Communications Act provides no specific guidance for determining when the Commission is empowered to regulate network practices or the standards by which industry performance is to be judged. Rather, the Act simply directs the FCC to regulate in the "public interest" and exhorts it to "encourage the larger and more effective use" of electromagnetic communication.[4] Indeed, the Act nowhere gives the Commission any express power to regulate networks although, as we have explained elsewhere, the agency's "ancillary jurisdiction" is probably sufficiently broad to encompass the types of regulations considered in this book.[5]

Workable Criteria

That specific criteria are difficult to come by, however, does not mean they cannot be developed. Necessarily, any set of standards will be controversial, because no source is indisputably both authoritative and precise. Nevertheless, careful examination of economic principles, First Amendment values, the Communications Act, and the Commission's precedents suggests that three widely agreed upon standards constitute workable criteria by which to measure television network commercial practices and FCC regulations affecting them. We propose, then, to assess FCC regulations of network structure and behavior by the extent to which they further the values of competition, diversity, and localism.

Basic Principles

Certain fundamental principles emerge from all three sources. Rehearsing them at the outset will help focus the issues. First, there is no reason to value, for its own sake, a reduction in television network size. As explained above, networking is an efficient method of supplying television programs to viewers and the simple fact that networks "dominate" the industry, in the sense that the majority of programs are produced for and distributed by networks, is neither surprising nor threatening. The number of networks and the relationships among them may substantially affect the Commission's economic and social policy goals, but the fact of networking does not.

Second, the elastic prescriptions of the Act quoted above are specific on one fundamental point completely consistent with economic and First Amendment values: the Commission's exclusive concern is the well-being of television viewers. In concrete terms, this means that the utility of a Commission policy should not be measured by the value it confers upon stations, advertisers, networks, or program producers. Certainly these entities perform valuable services insofar as they serve the public interest. Their welfare, however, apart from any effect they have on viewers' desires, interests, and rights, is not a criterion by which to judge the FCC's performance. In this respect, the Communications Act adopts a general principle of economic theory, fully consistent with First Amendment values, that business organizations are valued instrumentally, not intrinsically.

Finally, a fundamental First Amendment principle, embodied in the specific language and general structure of the Communications Act, is that neither the legality nor the utility of FCC regulations is to be judged according to the content, format, or subjective quality of the programs whose exhibition they stimulate or retard. The Act specifically forbids the Commission to engage in censorship, except for the limited purpose of banning obscene or indecent programs.[6] Further, the basic structure of the Act, as understood by the Commission and the courts, rests upon the premise that programming decisions are to be made by station licensees, not a majority of FCC commissioners.[7]

These fundamental policies, all consistent with each of the economic, social, and statutory goals the Commission must pursue, specify the issue we confront in searching for criteria by which to evaluate FCC regulation of network economic behavior. The question to be considered is what content-neutral criteria, which are also indifferent to the existence or success per se of networks, measure the contribution of Commission regulations to the well-being of viewers. We believe three such criteria exist.

Competition

Promoting competition within broadcast markets has long been a goal of the Commission and is probably the measure of FCC performance most readily accepted. The essential structure of the Communications Act rests heavily on the concept that what is broadcast and how the broadcasting business is organized and conducted should be determined principally by the forces of competition.[8]

Moreover, improving competition within the television industry also achieves many ends that are conducive to realizing First Amendment values and that are also desirable results of achieving economic efficiency. Under competitive conditions, the number, quality, content, and cost of programs are determined by impersonal marketplace forces rather than by the desires of a central government agency or a small number of firms. Reliance on competition among stations, networks, and program suppliers for consumers' patronage reflects the belief that, in general, the mix of programs that results from this competition will correspond closely to that mix desired by viewers.[9] Moreover, reliance on competition permits the profit-maximizing instincts of individual market participants to adapt and respond more flexibly and efficiently to changing consumer demands or changing technology and reduces the need to rely on more cumbersome or less responsive governmental agency choices.[10]

In the television industry, competition cannot produce strict economic efficiency because of the intractable problems of pricing this public good. Nor can competition alone produce access to all forums at the lowest possible cost, a desirable outcome suggested by First Amendment values, because of the absence of a market system for allocating the electromagnetic spectrum. Within these limits, however, promotion of competition within the television industry allows consumers to be the ultimate arbiters of what programs are boadcast.

An argument can be made that competition is the single criterion by which FCC regulations of network behavior should be measured. Certainly most economic policies that might be advocated are protected by competition. Further, insofar as the economic regulation of nonbroadcast media in this country can be said to rest on a coherent principle, that principle seems to be reliance on competition. The print media, for example, are largely left to develop in an economic environment regulated only by laws, such as the antitrust statutes, that apply to industrial firms generally. Lawmakers in the United States appear to have accepted the proposition that competition among writers and publishers for reader attention, and between the print media and other industries for the physical inputs necessary to satisfy reader demand, is generally sufficient to attain economic conditions compatible with freedom of expression. Thus we do not find a clamor for regulation of the book or paper production markets, for no one would complain that—

even when they behave competitively—these markets allocate too little paper to books and too much to matches or produce too few books urging adoption of the Equal Rights Amendment or that too few or too many book publishers emerge from such a system.

Nevertheless, diversity and localism are frequently suggested as additional or alternative criteria by which FCC economic regulations should be judged. This apparent paradox may be resolved, we think, by considering, in light of what has been said, precisely what those terms might signify. Properly understood, each can describe an additional, appropriate criterion by which to assess the Commission's performance.

Diversity

Federal courts have frequently agreed with the Commission that diversity is an objective the agency should pursue in regulating the broadcast industry.[11] The term is used to describe the goal of increasing the number and types of programs produced by different suppliers and broadcast to viewers by different firms. Diversity, so understood, contributes to viewers' enjoyment of television by increasing choices, thus making the medium useful to persons with varying desires and satisfying a larger number of viewer needs.

Put in such broad terms, the goal of diversity must seem as unobjectionable as that of promoting competition. Unlike competition, however, no single, accepted method of measuring diversity exists. We might well agree that diversity is desirable, but disagree substantially on what that value represents and how its advancement is to be measured.

The concept of diversity has three different but related dimensions: the types of programs; the sources of programs; and the number of choices or outlets available to viewers at any one time. Conceivably, the extent to which a Commission regulation furthers diversity could be measured by its contribution to each of these dimensions. A preferable alternative, however, is to measure whether the regulation fosters diversity by increasing the number of outlets, and therefore the number of viewing options, available to the public.

Measuring attainment of the goal of diversity by the criterion of increasing outlets is sensible in its own right because it is the most practical way to attain all the dimensions of diversity. The number of outlets available to viewers principally determines the extent to which producers and broadcasters will have incentives to offer programs of varying types.[12] For example, if a

program appeals only to 10 percent of potential viewers, a broadcaster in a
one-station market probably has little incentive to offer it; the same firm in a
ten-station market likely will find that program quite attractive. Further, the
opportunities for different producers or different broadcasters to gain access
to the television system necessarily are reduced where the number of outlets
is reduced.

Measuring diversity by the number of viewing options available also
avoids fundamental difficulties with the competing alternatives. If the goal
of diversity is measured by whether more or fewer program producers gain
air time, then the Commission can succeed only by promulgating regulations
that grant access to one producer at the expense of another. Such choices
can only be arbitrary. Further, such decisions do not increase the number of
choices available to viewers at any one time, and consequently give the
preferred producer no incentive to offer programs different from those
submitted by the disfavored. Measuring diversity by whether new or different programs are offered is inconsistent with the view that FCC regulations
should be content neutral.

In sum, diversity is an appealing criterion by which to measure FCC
economic regulation of the television industry so long as the unit of measurement employed is the number of outlets, or viewing options, available to
viewers at one time. Indeed, increasing viewers' options will ordinarily be
the best practical method to increase the other dimensions of diversity, types
of programs and sources of programs, and frequently will be the only
available way to do so.

Localism

No one can hope to evaluate the Commission's regulation of television
network commercial practices without coming to grips with a third criterion,
the standard of localism. Perhaps no shibboleth is uttered more frequently
in consideration of network regulations than that the television system must
satisfy the values of localism. Yet one must search long and hard for a
working definition of localism that does not reduce to the tautology that
everything not done by networks serves the goal of localism. Assuming that
plaintive appeals to promote localism are not simply disguised arguments
that regulations inhibiting networks are justified in themselves, we can
discern two dominant notions underlying the many specific varied uses of
the term.

Occasionally, localism is employed to express the view that individual rather than collective choice ought to lie at the center of decision making with respect to the nature and content of the programs that are shown. This version of localism is invoked to justify policies preferring programs that are responsive to the tastes and desires of viewers residing in the community within which programs are broadcast.[13] For apparently similar reasons, a policy favoring localism has been offered as support for the proposition that it is preferable to have program-selection decisions made by a broadcaster who resides in the community that will receive the broadcasts rather than by someone who lives outside the area.[14]

At other times, however, the concept of localism seems to reflect a view that values the identity of a community rather than the notion of individual choice. In some cases, localism has been measured by the extent to which the topic of a program is concerned exclusively with the community immediately surrounding a television transmitter, the number of local political issues aired, or the amount of air time afforded to local interest groups or their leaders.[15] Similarly, localism may reflect a desire that small cities and rural areas retain identities distinct from larger nearby metropolitan areas.[16]

These two views of localism are not entirely compatible. For example, individuals in a community may often prefer programs concerning national news or based upon international themes over local news or entertainment fare that features local talent or is recorded in the community. In evaluating FCC regulation according to the criterion of its contribution to localism, it thus seems helpful to consider localism as in fact representing two distinct policies. First, what we may describe as the "individual localism" criterion evaluates Commission regulations by the extent to which they permit more viewers (or more stations) to make more individual choices regarding what is broadcast. The second version, referred to here as the "community localism" criterion, values Commission regulations that lead to the broadcast of programs of limited geographical scope or interest.

For the sake of providing a more complete analysis, we propose to examine the extent to which FCC network regulation does or can advance either version of localism. Candor and completeness in judging these issues, however, requires that we confess our inability to understand what positive values the "community localism" criterion reflects. Certainly no economic policy suggests that the production or distribution of goods should be strictly confined to limited geopolitical areas. Nor is any First Amendment value of which we are aware involved in such questions as whether the settings of novels are located in readers' neighborhoods or whether books and magazines are distributed and sold nationally. Nor does any provision of the

Communications Act state or imply that programs set in their viewers' hometowns are to be preferred over those that are not.

Nevertheless, either view of localism can be addressed by our diversity criterion. Undoubtedly, increasing the number of outlets available to viewers is the most efficacious method of enhancing individual choice. Moreover, the availability of programs oriented to local tastes should be increased by expanding outlets, simply because the chances are thereby increased that offering local fare will provide a competitive advantage. Attempts can still be made, however, to measure separately attainment of both localism goals.

Conclusions

To evaluate any governmental regulation of commercial television network structure and behavior requires a set of criteria against which to measure network economic practices and rules proscribing or prescribing certain practices. Although widespread agreement does or should exist that network regulations should pursue three fundamental goals—economic efficiency, an economic environment conducive to the enjoyment of First Amendment freedoms, and observance of the policies established by the Communications Act—for a variety of reasons no criteria exist that can measure unequivocally the extent to which regulation furthers these goals.

We believe, nevertheless, that three criteria have a paramount claim to acceptance. We would assess the efficacy of regulations by inquiring whether they (1) promote competition, as that term is commonly understood, within broadcast markets; (2) increase diversity, as measured by increasing the number of viewing options available to members of the public at any one time; and (3) further "individual localism," i.e., permit more viewers or more stations to make more individual choices regarding what is broadcast. Put another way, we conclude that no government regulation of network business practices or organization is defensible if, in the absence of that regulation, viewers would then receive the maximum number of signals consistent with any limitations imposed by the physical properties of the electromagnetic spectrum and the need to dedicate parts of the spectrum to competing uses; the industry would operate within that allocation system in a competitive fashion; and influence over program choice would be wielded by the largest number of viewers and stations.

As we demonstrate in our analyses of actual and proposed regulations, our choice of criteria deliberately omits some values or goals that the

Commission, its supporters, and its critics have embraced in the past. For example, for the reasons stated above, we do not believe regulation of network practices can be defended plausibly on the grounds that it properly reallocates profits among stations, networks, and program suppliers or that it favors some producers or types of program over others or that it reduces the size of network schedules, audience levels, or profits. Defensible FCC policies may have one or more of these effects, but the existence of those consequences should not be treated as reasons to favor or reject those policies.

4 Existing and Proposed Regulations of Television Network Structure and Behavior

Whether additional commercial television networks will emerge and whether additional network growth will substantially modify the dominant positions presently occupied by ABC, CBS, and NBC cannot be predicted with assurance. In large measure, the answers to these questions depend upon future technological developments, the level of advertiser and viewer demand for television programs, and whether the FCC is willing and able to reduce the remaining entry barriers confronting potential new networks. All these future occurrences, none of which can be predicted confidently, will affect the prospects for new networks.

It is quite predictable, however, that whatever the state of competition among networks in the future, questions will arise concerning the extent to which the Commission should regulate their behavior. For, if nothing else is certain, the existence of economies of scale assures that networking will be the dominant organizational form in television, even in the technologically diverse environment likely to prevail a decade from now.

To determine how the Federal Communications Commission should react to pleas for restrictions on network commercial practices requires, first of all, an analysis of how the FCC has responded in the past. The following exposition of the Commission's existing rules and proposals to add to them is intended to provided a basis upon which to answer three questions suggested by our previous discussion: Do existing rules meet our criteria, given an industry in which FCC policies limit entry by additional networks? Should the content or coverage of these rules be modified if entry barriers confronting new networks are relaxed? Whatever the future conditions surrounding additional networks may be, should the FCC adopt or consider additional or different regulations?

FCC Regulation to Date[1]

Evolution of Rules Governing Television
Network Practices

Over the past four decades the Commission has promulgated a number of
rules governing the relations between television networks and their affiliates
and program suppliers. The majority of these rules derive from the Chain
Broadcasting Report of 1941, in which the FCC adopted, for the first time,
rules regulating network-affiliate relations in radio. The Commission applied these rules to television in 1946 without detailed reconsideration of the
bases for the rules or their utility for the new medium.[2] Indeed, in 1946
television networks existed only in rudimentary form.[3] Other rules were
added after the Barrow Report was completed in the fall of 1957, culminat-
ing a two-year FCC study of television network dominance. Finally, the
most recent rules, now almost ten years old, largely emerged from the
Commission's network program procurement study of the 1960s, and primarily address the dominant networks' relationships with program suppliers.

The majority of the Commission's network regulations attempt to limit
the perceived ability of the major networks to exact from their affiliates or
program suppliers onerous contract terms that may also entrench whatever
advantages existing networks enjoy over potential competitors. We describe these rules largely in the order in which they were promulgated, along
with brief summaries of the rationales offered when the rules were adopted.

1. *Term of Affiliation*
Network affiliation contracts may not bind a station to a network for
longer than two years. The Chain Broadcasting Report stopped the practice, which prevailed in the later 1930s, of negotiating for five-year affiliation
terms. The Commission concluded that lengthy terms hindered the growth
of alternative networks and prevented a station licensee from following its
conception of the public interest. Lowering the maximum term to two years
was designed to increase licensee accessibility to other program sources.

2. *Exclusive Affiliation*
Agreements between networks and their affiliates may not prevent these
stations from broadcasting programs of another network. The rule was
adopted in 1941 because the Commission believed such agreements deterred competition among networks, denied licensees freedom of choice in

programming, and restricted advertisers' choices of rates and coverage. The inability of NBC and CBS affiliates to broadcast the 1939 baseball World Series, carried by the Mutual Broadcast System, was noted as a particular instance of the harm the Commission intended to prevent.

3. *Territorial Exclusivity*
Another regulation that originated in the Chain Broadcasting Report provides that an affiliate may not prevent another station in the same geographical area from broadcasting network programs not taken by that affiliate. The Commission stated that it was not "in the public interest for the listening audience in an area to be deprived of network programs not carried by one station where other stations in that area are ready and willing to broadcast the program." A 1955 modification of the rule limits a television affiliate's permissible "right of first call" to the community designated in the station's license.

4. *Option Time*
Contract provisions that grant networks "options" to affiliates' time for certain portions of the broadcast day are prohibited. The CBS radio network pioneered the use of option clauses in which stations, as a condition of gaining affiliation, guaranteed to make certain amounts of specific station time available for network broadcasts, if the network chose to use it. The Chain Broadcasting Report concluded such clauses should be banned because they might present obstacles to the formation of new networks or hinder stations in developing local programming. This conclusion was altered in the Commission's Supplemental Report, however, and networks were permitted to acquire limited options in certain specified time periods, provided that at least 56 days' notice was given before any option was exercised. In 1957, the Barrow Report argued that all option clauses in television network affiliation agreements should be prohibited as contrary to the public interest, but in 1959 the Commission determined they were necessary for successful network operation and thus rejected the recommendation. Four years later, however, the Commission reversed its position and completely banned option time in network television, concluding that the adverse consequences of option clauses outweighed any benefits.

5. *The Right to Reject*
The network-affiliate contract must permit the station to reject programs offered or contracted for if the station reasonably believes the program is

unsatisfactory, unsuitable, or contrary to the public interest, or if the station wishes to substitute a program it believes is of greater importance. As the Commission explained when adopting it in 1941, the rule reenforces the station's nondelegable duty to determine whether the public interest is served by its programming.

6. *Dual Network Operation*

Stations may not affiliate with a network that simultaneously operates more than one network of television stations, unless there is no substantial overlap in the territories served by the stations comprising the networks. This ruled was adopted originally for the specific purpose of reducing the market power NBC enjoyed as a consequence of operating two networks, the "Red" and the "Blue," during the 1930s. The Chain Broadcasting Report concluded that NBC obtained a competitive advantage over other existing networks and protection against future competition by virtue of operating two networks. Further, NBC's dual networking was believed to give NBC undue control over its affiliated stations because the affiliation contracts did not specify whether a station was affiliated with the Red or Blue network.

Fearing the unfair effects of a "forced sale" of one of the networks, however, the Commission indefinitely suspended the rule in its 1941 Supplemental Report, noting that "separate ownership of what are now the Red and Blue networks of NBC is so generally recognized to be desirable that we believe a separation will soon occur without the spur of a legal mandate." After NBC sold its Blue network in 1943, the dual networking prohibition was readopted and was incorporated in the Chain Broadcasting Rules applied to television in 1946.

7. *Network Ownership of Stations*

Although the Chain Broadcasting Report questioned whether networks should be allowed to own stations at all, the Commission adopted two less restrictive rules. One prohibited networks from owning more than one station in a market, while the other forbade networks from owning any station in a locality where the existing stations are so few or of such unequal desirability that competition would be substantially restrained by network ownership. The former prohibition has since been subsumed in FCC ownership rules applicable to all station owners, while the latter retains its original form, but has not had significant consequences for television networks.

8. *Control of Station Rates by Networks*

The final rule emanating from the Chain Broadcasting Report provides that a network may not prevent or hinder a station from altering its rates for the sale of broadcast time for nonnetwork programming. NBC had argued that its affiliates ought not compete with the network for national advertisers, but the Commission disagreed.

9. *Regulation of Compensation Plans*

The Commission has never adopted any formal rules regulating or limiting the manner in which networks compensate their affiliated stations for carrying (or "clearing," in industry parlance) network programs. Nevertheless, the Commission has accomplished some regulation of compensation plans through interpretation of its rules banning exclusive affiliation and option time and ensuring affiliates' rights to reject network programs. These interpretations implement policies advocated by the 1957 Barrow Report.

In 1958 the Commission concluded that a television network practice of regularly and directly associating an affiliate's compensation rate with its levels of program clearance would violate the prohibition on exclusive affiliation. Later, the Commission held that a television network compensation plan in which "the average hourly rate of compensation varies greatly or is heavily influenced by the number of hours taken" violates the right to reject and option time rules. Under these interpretations, all graduated compensation plans are not illegal. Rather, the ruling proscribes only those plans containing what the Commission described as "an extreme sliding-scale formula which severely penalizes the affiliate which does not clear the bulk" of the network's programs.

10. *Representation of Affiliates in the National Spot Market.*

Networks are not permitted to represent their affiliates in the sale of national advertising time. This rule, recommended in the Barrow Report, is based on the belief that networks and affiliates compete for national advertisers and that networks therefore would have a conflict of interest if they represented both themselves and their affiliates. The regulation's premise, that affiliates and networks compete in advertising sales, is identical to the rationale underlying the ban on networks controlling their affiliates' station rates.

11. *Network Syndication and Procurement Practices*

Networks are forbidden to engage in domestic syndication of any program or foreign syndication of independently produced programs, and also to obtain any financial or proprietary rights in the exhibition, distribution, or use of programs produced by others except for the exclusive right to network exhibition in the United States. Both the syndication and financial interest rules, promulgated in 1970 after lengthy investigation of network program procurement practices, were designed to remedy perceived abuses of market power by the television networks in purchasing programs for network exhibition. The Commission anticipated that these rules would reduce network control over alternative program sources and ameliorate an imbalance in bargaining power between networks and program producers.

12. *Prime Time Access Rule*
    Also promulgated in 1970, this rule provides that television stations in the top fifty markets that are affiliated with a network may exhibit no more than three hours of network (or syndicated off-network) entertainment programming during prime time (7 to 11 P.M., Eastern time). Although many explanations have been offered for the rule, it was designed, at least in part, to increase the competition offered to network programs by producers of first-run syndicated (nonnetwork) programs and to reduce the market power networks exercise over producers of network-quality programs.

13. *One Affiliation per Station*
    In markets where two stations are affiliated with networks, and one or more other commercial stations with "reasonably comparable facilities" are in operation but are not affiliated with any network, one or both of the affiliated stations may have a "secondary" affiliation with the third network. A rule promulgated in 1971 prohibits such affiliated stations from taking prime–time programs and weekend sports events from their secondary network unless the unaffiliated station has first been offered the programs. The rule was designed, with the advent of the Prime Time Access Rule, to prevent a (VHF) station with dual affiliation from broadcasting programs from its secondary network while an unaffiliated (UHF) station in the market remained unable to acquire a network affiliation. The practical effect of the rule is to force the secondary network to affiliate with the UHF station.

14. *Network Ownership of Cable Systems*
    Networks are forbidden to own cable television systems, although the Commission recently granted CBS a limited waiver from this prohibition. The rule, adopted in 1970, emerged from a general FCC review of its

regulatory oversight of the cable industry. The Commission has never provided any detailed statement of the rule's purposes or probable effects, beyond the assertion that it "was designed to insure vigorous competition among the mass media and to obtain for the public the greatest possible diversity of control over local mass communications media."

Definition of "Network"Employed

To understand fully the various FCC rules respecting television network comercial practices requires knowledge of the different types of entities subject to those rules. Many of these rules rest upon theories that assume an environment in which a few dominant networks are able to engage in practices that are not tempered by competition from numerous rivals. Nevertheless, the Commission's present rules adopt widely differing definitions of those entities that constitute a "network."

Limitation on Traditional, Interconnected Networks

All the rules described in the preceding section share one feature—they apply only to networks that electronically interconnect over-the-air television broadcast licensees or to affiliates of such networks. Thus, program distributors that use the postal system are not covered by the rules, nor are networks of cable systems, even if the latter distribute programs via terrestrial microwave or satellite. Networks using the newer technologies will be covered or exempt from these rules depending on the status of the outlets they employ for local distribution. For example, MDS systems are regulated as common carriers, not broadcast stations, so a network of MDS outlets will not be subject to any of these rules. A network of STV stations that offers identical programming, however, will be covered because STV stations are broadcast licensees.

Pre-1970 Rules

Most of the FCC rules governing the network-affiliate relationship, and all the network rules promulgated before 1970, apply to all networks of interconnected broadcast stations, whatever their size. Specifically, the first ten rules and regulations described in the preceding section apply to any network interconnecting two or more broadcasting licensees. This designation of a network tracks the definition of "chain broadcasting" contained in section 3(p) of the Communications Act of 1934.[4]

The Chain Broadcasting Report considered the argument that only affiliation contracts of large, national networks should be regulated. The report concluded, however, that all interconnected networks, no matter how small, should be governed by its rules. It argued, first, that operations of regional networks may, with respect to an individual station, a community, or a region, "operate to foster a local monopoly and to impair station operation in the public interest just as effectively and as intensively as similar practices on a national scale." Second, the report contended that to exempt smaller regional networks "would open the way for [arrangements inconsistent with the rules] to become the usual pattern of network affiliation." If this occurred, the Report argued, national networks might "surround themselves with a group of associated regional networks" employing arrangements that otherwise would be prohibited. The Commission also concluded that affiliates of regional networks "should retain their freedom of operation in the public interest as fully as stations affiliated with national networks."

Network Program Supply Rules

The prime-time access, financial interest, and syndication rules, promulgated in 1970, employ a very different definition of "network." These rules apply only to persons or firms offering "interconnected program service on a regular basis for 15 or more hours per week to at least 25 affiliated television licensees in 10 or more states." The manner in which this definition developed sheds some light on the Commission's purposes.

In 1965 the Commission proposed the adoption of three new rules, which later evolved into the prime-time access, financial interest, and syndication rules. The proposals were said to be designed to reduce network dominance in the program procurement market. The operative term employed by the Commission in delineating the scope of the proposed rules was "network television licensee," which was defined in subparagraph (a):

> As used in this section the term "network television licensee" means a television station licensee (or any person controlling, controlled by or under common control with such licensee) which engages in chain broadcasting. For the purposes of this section, chain broadcasting means the furnishing of programs to a substantial number of television broadcast stations on a daily basis for a substantial number of hours per day.

By defining "chain broadcasting" as furnishing programs to a substantial number of television broadcast stations on a daily basis for a substantial number of hours a day, the Commission departed deliberately from the broader statutory definition and from that adopted in the 1941 Report on Chain Broadcasting. Indeed, a close reading of the Commission's Notice of Proposed Rulemaking makes it clear that it intended that the three proposed rules would apply only to ABC, CBS, and NBC. In describing the problem addressed by the proposed rules, the Commission repeatedly referred to the "three national network corporations," and all data cited to demonstrate the existence of network dominance relate solely to these three firms.

In its conclusion the Commission noted:

> At the present time there is an undue concentration of control in *the three network corporations* over television programs available to the public. . . .
> Furthermore, this intense concentration of power decreases the competitive opportunity for independent program producers. Under present practices they must, in practical effect, deal with *the three network corporations* on their terms or give up hope of producing programs for exhibition on television networks.

Finally, the Commission invited comments with respect to the definition of networks, stressing that its proposed definition would not impede the development of additional networks:

> Since the proposed rule defines chain broadcasting as the distribution of programs to a substantial number of stations during a substantial period of the day (and we specifically seek comments on the precise terms of this definition), and since, in addition, the [prime-time access portion of the] rule would not affect any person distributing less than 14 hours a week between 6 and 11 PM of programming he controlled, the restrictions in the rule clearly would not impede the development of any proposed additional networks.

In 1970 the Commission formally adopted the prime-time access, syndication, and financial interest rules, but the language in the 1965 proposed rules limiting their application to networks that furnish programs to a substantial number of stations on a daily basis for a substantial number of hours per day was deleted. Instead, the rule was made applicable to every "television network," a term left undefined.

Despite the apparent broadening of the definition of a network, a close reading of the *Report and Order* announcing the adoption of the rules reveals that the bases of the Commission's concerns were limited to the practices of the three national networks. Thus at the outset the Commission noted that "the facts which propel us to action are relatively simple and, we believe, quite compelling. There are only three national television networks." As in the Notice, the Commission again referred repeatedly to the "three national networks," and all data presented in support of the rules related solely to the three national networks.

Shortly after their adoption, the rules were amended to apply only to networks of a certain size, as described above. The amendment was adopted at the request of several petitioners who urged that the term "network" be defined "so as to include only the three national networks." In responding to the request of the Hughes Sports Network, the Commission noted that there was "no 'sound and evident' reason" to prohibit stations subject to the rule from broadcasting "both a full major network prime time schedule and programs of regional or lesser national networks. . . ." The FCC emphasized that its desire to encourage the development of additional networks required that the scope of the three rules be limited to the existing national networks:

> Encouragement of the development of additional networks to supplement or compete with existing networks is a desirable objective and has long been the policy of this Commission. Hence we have redefined the term "network" in the Prime Time Access Rule to apply only to major national television networks. This will remove any doubt that our actions are intended to encourage the competitive development of additional networks as well as other alternate program sources.

A review of all the proceedings in this docket reveals three reasons for the limitation of these rules to major networks. First, the Commission believed that the nature of the problem addressed by the rules did not require that all networks be subject to them. The rules adopted in 1970 were designed to reduce "network dominance" of the program production process and prime-time television programming. Obviously, this "dominance" did not involve small regional networks but was exerted, in the Commission's view, solely by the three national networks. The conclusion that smaller networks should be free to adopt practices forbidden to the dominant networks was directly contrary to the position taken in the Chain Broadcasting Report. In part, the reversal was due to an additional consideration that led the FCC to restrict the coverage of its 1970 rules. The Commission hoped these rules would enhance the prospects for additional networks, but recognized that their application to emerging networks might diminish these prospects rather than enhance them. Finally, jurisdictional considerations troubled the commission. Whether the FCC possessed the authority to regulate the networks directly was quite unsettled in 1970.[5] The rules regulating network-affiliate relations, which applied to all over-the-air networks, had been justified at least in part by citing the Commission's jurisdiction over affiliated stations rather than the networks themselves. The financial interest and syndication rules, however, were to apply formally only to network behavior. In the Commission's view, its jurisdiction over enactment of such rules was more clearly established with respect to the major networks because they were the "key elements in chain broadcasting."

One Affiliation per Station Rule

The "one affiliation per station" (or "forced affiliation") rule incorporates two other definitions of network organization. Formally, the rule prevents certain affiliated stations from taking programs from certain networks with which the station is not primarily affiliated, unless certain conditions have been met. For purposes of the rule, a station is "affiliated" if it has a "regular affiliation with one of the three national television networks." Put another way, for purposes of determining which stations are primarily affiliated with one network, and therefore may not maintain extensive secondary network affiliations, only ABC, CBS, and NBC may constitute "networks." Networks whose programs are affected by the rule are defined differently, and include any "national organization" that distributes programs "for a substantial part of each broadcast day to television stations in all parts of the United States, generally via interconnection facilities."

It appears that no detailed consideration was given to the scope of this rule. Rather, it was assumed from the outset that only ABC, CBS, and NBC affiliation practices were to be considered, because at that time only those entities were involved in the practices addressed by the rule.

Neither in its 1970 notice proposing the rule, nor its 1971 decision adopting it, did the Commission explain why the rule was drafted to apply only to the three national networks. In its Memorandum Opinion and Order responding to several petitions for reconsideration, however, the Commission finally addressed the issue directly.

In its Petition for Reconsideration, NBC argued that the rule "illegally discriminates against [the three national] networks, since other program suppliers (syndicated program suppliers, or other 'networks' such as the Hughes Sports Network or regional networks) are not subject to the same restrictions, but can sell programs to whomever they choose." The Commission rejected this contention, however, noting:

> The three national networks are sufficiently 'different' from such other sources—for example, in their method of program distribution and provision of advertising support for broadcasting, and in the crucial importance of their programming to the viability of stations outside of the largest markets (particularly to UHF stations)—to warrant treatment which is, to a degree, disparate. Moreover, as the proponents of the rule point out, an administrative agency is not obligated to deal with all of the aspects of a problem at one time. As some of these other sources approach similarity in the three national networks in some of the pertinent respects—for example, the national sale by syndicators of some of the commercial slots in the programs they furnish to stations—it may be appropriate to adopt similar regulations as to them.

Cable System Ownership Ban

By the time it promulgated the network-cable system ownership rule, the Commission apparently had exhausted its capacity to define networks. The rule simply prohibits cable system ownership by a "national television network (such as ABC, CBS, or NBC)." How or why this limited, firm-specific definition was derived or adopted has never been explained.[6] Perhaps a firm virtually identical to, for example, ABC might be treated properly as a "network (such as ABC . . .)," but in practice this definition can only mean and has only meant that only three specific corporate entities are subject to the rule.

Summary

The preceding review of the varying definitions of "network" employed in the Commission's network regulations points to several preliminary conclusions. Obviously, the Commission has not employed a single, consistent definition of "network" and, consequently, the scope of existing rules varies substantially. In part these varying definitions reflect different resolutions of the question whether regulations should encompass smaller as well as dominant networks. In part, they reflect doubts about the extent of Commission jurisdiction.

To some extent, however, the use of different definitions results from the fact that the Commission's network rules do not embody a coherent, overall policy toward network behavior, but rather a disparate collection of separate provisions, each enacted to deal with a specific "abuse" and written only with the goal of changing the behavior of those already identified as engaged in the practice to be corrected. Thus the rules do not consistently define the types of network behavior the Commission generally wishes to prevent or deter, but, rather, describe only specific instances of behavior the Commission has found inappropriate. Finally, the fact that all the rules apply only to networks of interconnected, over-the-air, broadcast stations surely promises to generate substantial controversy in the future as networks using other methods of local distribution continue to develop.

Repeal of Radio Network Rules

As noted earlier, many of the FCC rules regulating television network-affiliate relationships were originally designed in 1941 to regulate radio networks. Those rules were simply extended to television in 1946, before the development of substantial television networks, on the apparent assumption that whatever television network forms arose, it would be sensible to govern them in the same manner as radio networks.

The historical connection between the radio and television rules is itself sufficient justification for examining more carefully the Commission's 1977 decision to repeal most of its then-applicable radio network rules.[7] It is especially noteworthy that the Commission did not state that the principles behind the Chain Broadcasting rules were misguided. Rather, the agency asserted that "tremendously changed circumstances" in the economic environment in which radio networks existed made the rules unnecessary.

The changes in circumstances were great indeed, and the Commission listed the most significant as follows:

1. *Numbers of stations.* There were fewer than 1000 stations operating in 1941 and the Chain Broadcasting Report itself dealt with only 660, but over 8000 radio stations were on the air in 1977.

2. *Major markets.* Of ninety-two cities with a population over 100,000 in 1941, fewer than fifty had three or more full-time radio stations and fewer than thirty had four or more. By 1977, in contrast, ninety-eight of the top one hundred markets had more than ten radio and television stations.

3. *Increased national services.* There were only four national radio networks in 1941, of which NBC owned two. By 1977, five companies operated

ten radio networks (the FCC had waived its dual network rules to permit these developments), and these figures did not include AP and UPI radio services or occasional networks.

4. *Decreased economic importance of networks.* Networks accounted for 46 percent of radio revenue in 1941 and in 1938 earned profits of $4.3 million. By 1975, the network profits were only $2.6 million.

5. *Changed nature of service.* In 1941, network radio consisted largely of entertainment programs lasting a half-hour or longer. By 1977 it consisted mostly of news and informational material presented in segments of five minutes or less.

Because of these changes, and also because of fear that some of the Chain Broadcasting Rules might deter innovative new radio networks, the Commission repealed the bulk of the rules including those regulating exclusive affiliation, term of affiliation, option time (noting that even though substantial option time was available to radio networks, few availed themselves of it), right to reject network programs, and network control of station rates.

In addition, the rule limiting network ownership of radio stations was repealed. The Commission noted that the part of the rule preventing a network from owning two stations in the same market was covered by ownership rules applicable to all entities. Further, the Commission concluded that the other part of the network ownership rule, which prohibited a network from owning a station in a market where facilities were too few or of unequal desirability, addressed a situation that was now unlikely to occur and could, in any event, be handled on a case-by-case basis.

The Commission was equally certain that the changed circumstances did not warrant any relaxation of the rule prohibiting affiliates from obtaining territorial exclusivity. ABC had argued the rule was unnecessary because network programming consists largely of short newscasts, similar programming is available from other sources, and it is usually impractical to offer others what an affiliate rejects. But the Commission found no reason to believe the rule was not needed and feared possible adverse consequences from its repeal. In particular, the Commission concluded that "the decline of relative network dominance is more likely to increase the need for [the] rule than to lessen it," presumably because the rule is designed to protect against exercise of market power by affiliated stations. Further, the Commission believed the rule contributed to making network programs widely available.

Finally, the Commission adopted a Statement of Policy in which it stressed two points. First, "licensees have an affirmative, non-delegable duty to choose independently all programming" they broadcast. Affiliation agreements should not infringe on this duty. Second, network programming "should be widely available, without undue restrictions on its availability."

The FCC's 1977 decision to release radio networks from most of the Commission's network-affiliate rules suggests that the Commission itself, at least in retrospect, understood the regulations to be at best useful temporary measures, designed either to correct imbalances in bargaining power between networks and their affiliates or to facilitate further network entry, and adapted only to a system where few networks exist because of transitory technological and legal constraints. The 1977 repeal, therefore, is further evidence that, in evaluating regulations of network commercial practices, one must be specific about the goals the Commission should pursue and the economic environment in which the rules would operate.

Additional Regulations Suggested or Contemplated by the Commission

The academic and popular literature on network broadcast economics contains so many suggestions for additional regulation of commercial television network practices that no single study could list, let alone analyze, them all. Two fairly recent events, however, suggest the types of additional regulations the Commission would most likely consider were the agency to attempt again to tame network dominance by reining in network practices. First, the Commission's 1977 Notice of Inquiry, initiating its latest study of network economic conduct, suggests some additional regulations of the network-affiliate relationship.[8] Second, consent decrees obtained between 1976 and 1980 by the Department of Justice in settling antitrust cases against ABC, CBS, and NBC impose several limitations, which go beyond existing FCC rules, on the contractual rights networks may obtain in purchasing programming from independent program suppliers.[9] Most provisions of these decrees are to be in effect for only a few years, but the Commission has expressed an interest in studying the desirability of adopting similar regulations, and several major program producers have earnestly pressed the FCC to do so.

The Network-Affiliate Relationship

Affiliation contracts, we have seen, are extensively regulated by the Commission. Further, it seems to be common ground among students of the network-affiliate relationship that the FCC should not attempt to regulate directly the amount of compensation networks pay their affiliates. For these reasons, there are few candidates for additional, possible regulations of affiliation practices. Nevertheless, the Commission expressed fears in its 1977 Notice that network programs might be occupying undue portions of affiliates' schedules and that compensation plans inadequately reward affiliates for their participation in networking. Three more specific areas of regulation were identified, each of which would increase Commission oversight of the process of clearing network programs.

Expansion of Network Schedules

The Commission might fear that the networks would expand their schedules in order to preempt station time that otherwise might be available to other competing networks. Two forms of regulation of network schedules are conceivable. One would follow the approach of the prime-time access rule, forbidding networks to supply programs to affiliates during certain times. The other would limit the hours of programming networks could offer per day, week, or year, leaving to network-affiliate bargaining the decision as to which time periods will be vacated.

Station Compensation Plans

The Commission has determined, as we have noted, that although it will not regulate the aggregate level of network compensation, it should limit the structure of compensation payments. The agency fears that if compensation per clearance rises with increases in total clearances, affiliates will be induced to clear programs they would otherwise reject. The FCC's premise is that the form of compensation can be regulated even though overall compensation is not controlled.

The Commission's 1977 Notice asked what effect existing graduated compensation plans have on stations' "independent discretion" and on the "ability of syndicators and other program suppliers to compete with the networks by dealing directly with affiliated stations." Although no specific rules were proposed, two types might respond to these fears of network foreclosure. One would ban graduated compensation plans altogether; another would place more specific limits on the permissible difference between average and marginal compensation.

Previewing of Network Programs

A recent specific complaint has been that the networks fail to give their affiliates sufficient opportunity to preview network programs, before their broadcast, to ascertain whether those programs are suitable for viewing in the affiliate's community. Two distinct policies may be implicated by network previewing practices. First, values of localism may be overridden if locally based affiliates are unable to prescreen program decisions made by national networks. Second, if affiliates are unable to preview network programs, the stations may lack sufficient information to bargain effectively with networks over the extent of, and compensation for, carriage of network programs. A specific proposal made to the FCC was to require networks to make previewing opportunities available to affiliates at least four weeks before the network broadcast of a program.[10]

The Network-Program Supplier Relationship

The entry of the Justice Department consent decree led the Commission to suggest in its 1977 Notice of Inquiry a renewed FCC interest in regulating the manner in which the dominant, conventional networks acquire programs. Three types of proposed regulations typify the concerns recently voiced.

The Scope of the Financial Interest and Syndication Rules
One issue frequently raised is whether the financial interest and syndication rules are sufficiently broad. Do, or should, the rules prohibit the networks from obtaining nonbroadcast rights to programs independently produced? For example, it has been asked whether the financial interest rule should prevent ABC, CBS, and NBC from acquiring the right to exhibit on a cable network a program acquired for the network's conventional distribution. Do, or should, the rules affect the manner in which stations owned by ABC, CBS, or NBC acquire syndicated programs? For example, should the stations owned by one network be permitted to acquire, as a group, syndicated programs produced for the prime-time access period?
As we shall see, the questions surrounding these rules are not mere issues of interpretation. Rather, they call for a reassessment of the rules' underlying purposes and economic effects.

Network ("in-house") Production
Most of the entertainment programs shown by ABC, CBS, and NBC are acquired from firms independent of the networks. Occasionally, however, these networks produce their own drama or comedy series or made-for-television motion pictures. A principal reason for the Justice Department

antitrust suit was to reduce or eliminate the extent of this "in-house" production.

Opponents claim that network in-house production is anticompetitive because it gives networks leverage in bargaining with independent producers. It is asserted that, because ABC, CBS, and NBC each combine the program purchasing power of many broadcast stations that are sheltered from competition, these networks can, if they choose, monopolize the business of producing television entertainment films. By engaging in some such production, and threatening to produce even more, it is contended that the networks could dictate onerous terms to independent producers or could exclude these firms arbitrarily from the production market.

Acquisition of Protective Network Rights

Contracts for network exhibition rights to television shows are typically lengthy and complex.[11] Questions have been raised concerning virtually every type of provision commonly found in these agreements. Most attention, however, has centered on provisions in network entertainment series contracts regarding options, exclusivity, and spin-off protection.[12]

Option clauses grant the networks the right to renew a series for another year at the expiration of one year's episodes. Frequently the initial program supply contract gives the network four to seven years of options. Most contracts also contain an exclusivity clause designed to prevent exhibition of a series' episodes on other networks or via syndication so long as the initial contracting network exercises its options to retain the series. Many program supply contracts provide the network some protection against a "spin-off" series (a program series built around a character initially developed or introduced in an earlier series) being exhibited on another network.

Critics have alleged that options, exclusivity, and spin-off protection, singly or collectively, facilitate monopolization by the dominant networks of the program supply business. These terms assertedly prevent producers from moving successful series to competing networks and allow the dominant networks to tie up most available program inventory. Further claims are that such provisions give networks undue control over the price of independently produced programs and the decisions whether to produce them and how they are to be distributed.

No one has yet suggested that these terms should be abolished entirely from contracts for the supply of network entertainment series. Many, however, have urged regulation that limits the number of options or the extent of exclusivity or spin-off protection networks can obtain. The consent decrees concluding the Justice Department antitrust suits contain such limits, although the specific provisions of the decrees do little more than codify existing practices.

Summary

When the list of existing FCC regulations is added to those recently proposed or considered, the number of controls to be evaluated is indeed great. In large measure, the remainder of our analysis seeks to explain how this apparent complexity can be simplified by paying careful attention to the economic principles that govern the system of commercial television networking and to the public policy criteria that should guide the FCC's response to allegations of network misbehavior or monopolization.

5   Economic Analysis of the Relationship between Networks and Their Affiliates

To appreciate the effects of the various Commission regulations of network affiliation contracts requires an understanding of the economics of the network-affiliate relationship. The specific examples discussed below are drawn from the actual practices of the dominant, conventional networks, but they describe a model that applies to the general phenomenon of linking a variety of scattered, local outlets in order to broadcast television programs widely.

The Organization of the Relationship

As noted at the outset, networks exist in a vertical economic relationship to local station outlets. Networks provide programs to broadcasters, cable systems, and other local program distributors who use these programs to provide an overall program schedule to offer to advertisers or viewers or both.

The relationship between the dominant, conventional television networks and their affiliated stations can be characterized in two equivalent ways. On the one hand, the networks can be described as buying access to the time of stations, paying for this time both in cash and by permitting stations to sell spots within and between programs to advertisers. Alternatively, one can think of stations as purchasing programs from the networks, paying for these programs by permitting the networks to sell advertising time within programs and to retain a portion of the resulting revenues.

Each network acquires from independent suppliers, or produces itself, programs that the network offers to its affiliates on terms agreed to in its affiliation contract. For programs of one-half hour of less, the network usually retains control of all advertising time within programs and the stations can sell all commercial time between programs. For longer programs, the stations also have available some time within programs, usually on the hour and the half-hour.[1] The time periods reserved for sale by affiliates are referred to as adjacencies.

The Significance of Direct
Compensation Payments

In addition to the revenues from advertising time that they sell themselves, stations also receive direct compensation from the network for the carriage (clearance) of network programs. On the average, network compensation amounts only to about 7 percent of the total revenues received by network affiliates.[2] For this reason, one could argue that the amount of compensation cannot be a substantial factor in an affiliate's decision whether to clear a network program.

The significance of station compensation becomes more apparent, however, if it is compared to profits rather than to revenues. If, in 1980, the networks had paid no compensation and other factors such as program clearances and advertising revenues had remained constant, affiliate profits would have been reduced by about one-third and network profits would have almost doubled.[3] Moreover, since a substantial amount of affiliates' time is occupied by nonnetwork programs, network compensation represents more than 7 percent of the revenue obtained when the affiliates carry network programs. In addition, because compensation is paid only for programs cleared in excess of a stated minimum (i.e., because compensation plans are somewhat graduated), average compensation is smaller than marginal compensation. In other words, once the minimum is exceeded, which it invariably is, network compensation represents more than 7 percent of total station receipts for each additional program carried.

Finally, network compensation differs from most other forms of station income because the network can potentially use compensation to distinguish among its affiliates. A network that wishes, for example, to raise compensation for only one of its stations would not do so by increasing the proportion of advertising time made available to affiliates, for in that case all affiliates would benefit. Instead, the network would increase the compensation it pays to that station, so *only* that station would gain. Station compensation thus provides a vehicle through which networks may treat different stations differently.

Contract Provisions Determining Compensation

Each of the three dominant, conventional networks employs a standard formula to calculate compensation for each of its affiliates.[4] Although occasionally an affiliate obtains some variation in the formula, bargaining generally takes place over the "network rate" to which the formula is applied.

Each ABC affiliation contract establishes a network station rate stated in dollars per hour. To determine compensation for the carriage of a given program, this rate is multiplied by a percentage depending on the time of day of the broadcast, by the fraction of an hour occupied by the program, and by the fraction of the length of all commercial availabilities occupied by network commercials. Each week, ABC deducts from the compensation due to a station an amount equal to 205 percent of the station's network rate.

The basic compensation formula for CBS affiliates differs from the ABC formula only in the percentages of the network rate paid for the carriage of programs during various time periods. CBS also deducts an amount equal to 205 percent of the station's rate each week, as well as any cooperative commercial payments.

NBC divides the broadcast day into rate periods; for example, prime time is a full-rate period and daytime is a 35-percent-rate period. These rates provide the basis for converting program hours into so-called equivalent hours. NBC converts the hours of network programs broadcast into equivalent hours by multiplying the former by the rate in effect at the time the program was broadcast. Thus, an hour of prime-time programming is one equivalent hour. NBC affiliates agree to waive compensation on the first twenty four equivalent hours broadcast each month. Each equivalent hour in excess of twenty four is multiplied by the network station rate, and NBC pays to the station a percentage of this product, typically amounting to one-third. The result is that the deductions for NBC affiliates are about eight times a station's hourly network rate per month, which is approximately the same as that for ABC and CBS.

These contract provisions establish the manner in which the dominant networks and their affiliates determine program clearances and the station compensation. Against this background, we can explain the economic forces at work in that bargaining process.

The Economics of Program
Clearance Decisions

The Affiliate Supply Schedule

In deciding the amount of time and the specific time periods to supply to a network, a station must compare the net revenue it can earn by supplying each time period to the network to what it can earn if it broadcasts nonnetwork material.[5] The affiliate's net revenue from exhibiting a network program, of course, is the sum of network compensation and the receipts the station receives from the sale of adjacencies. The net revenue from a nonnetwork program is equal to the revenue the station generates from selling commercial time minus the costs of acquiring rights to syndicated programs or producing its own shows.

The networks can influence the choices affiliates make by any or all of three methods: (1) adjusting network compensation for a network program; (2) altering the length of time for, and hence the receipts that can be obtained from, the sale of commercial adjacencies in or surrounding network programs; or (3) changing the programs the network offers in order to alter the value of those adjacencies. The following analysis takes as given the length of time allotted to commercial announcements between and within programs and the network program lineup, and we consider that the primary means networks use to obtain clearances is to vary one or more of the contract terms that determine station compensation. These terms are: (1) the network rate for any given time period; (2) the proportion of the network rate paid as compensation; and (3) the number of deductions taken. Since a given amount of compensation can be produced through various combinations of (1) and (2), the following section discusses only the dollar amount of compensation without regard to the manner in which it is derived.

From the viewpoint of the network seeking to "buy" clearances from its affiliates, it is possible to construct a "supply schedule of time offered" by each affiliate, showing the relationship between station compensation and the number of hours of network programs that the affiliate will clear. For each available network program, the affiliate calculates the level of network compensation at which it is just willing to clear the program, that is, the affiliate's "reservation price" for that particular program. The reservation price is that amount which, when added to the value of adjacencies, just equates the net revenue from a network program with that of its best nonnetwork program alternative. If network compensation exceeds the reservation price, the station will clear the network program, but if it is below that price the network program will be preempted in favor of nonnetwork material.

The reservation price will most likely differ among programs. For some network programs, the nonnetwork alternatives will be very unattractive because the costs of acquiring or producing these alternatives are high relative to the revenues they can generate. In these cases, the affiliate will prefer the network offering even at low network compensation rates. For other network programs, net revenues from nonnetwork alternatives will be high and network programs will be cleared only at a higher compensation rate. In principle, one can array programs according to the affiliate's reservation price starting with that program for which the reservation price is the lowest, followed by that with the next lowest reservation price, and so on until the array is completed with the program having the highest reservation price.

Table 5.1 illustrates a supply schedule of time for a hypothetical affiliate. Programs listed in the left-hand column are arrayed in ascending order of the station's reservation price, shown in the right-hand column. Thus, for example, the network compensation necessary to induce the affiliate to clear program A is 30, while it requires compensation of 40 to induce clearance of B.

Each affiliate has a schedule such as that in table 5.1. Identical programs will generate different advertising revenues for different stations depending principally on the size of the market each station serves. Therefore, affiliates in large markets will have higher reservation prices for each network program than affiliates in smaller markets, since the nonnetwork alternatives in the former will generate a higher net revenue than in the latter. Similarly, because one of the determinants of an affiliate's reservation price is the

Table 5.1   Affiliate's Supply Schedule

Network programs	Affiliate's reservation price (required compensation)
A	30
B	40
C	50
D	60

value of adjacencies, affiliates of the network with the most popular programs will be willing to clear a given program for smaller direct compensation than an affiliate of a weaker network.

Joint Clearance Determination

A network, of course, must determine whether it is willing to pay these affiliate reservation prices. In deciding how much it is willing to pay for a clearance, a network must calculate the addition to its revenues provided by the affiliate's clearance.

Once a program has been produced, an affiliation contract has been negotiated, and continuous interconnection arranged, a network can provide the program to an affiliate essentially without cost. The network therefore will seek to have the program carried on a station so long as compensation paid does not exceed the additional advertising revenues from having the program carried by that station. Naturally, however, the network will seek to pay less than this amount. Indeed, a network could not pay all of its advertising revenues as compensation since it would then be unable to cover its other costs such as program acquisition and station interconnection. Thus, for a network to be viable, a substantial number of affiliates must receive compensation lower than the maximum amount a network might be willing to pay to any given affiliate.

In table 5.2, column 4 repeats the figures from table 5.1 and shows the minimum compensation the hypothetical affiliate will accept to clear each network program (its reservation price). Column 5 reflects the maximum the hypothetical network is willing to pay for that clearance. For the sake of simplicity, it is assumed that each program cleared adds 55 to network revenue. In this example, it is in the interest of both the network and the affiliate to have only the network programs A, B, and C cleared. The network will not want to have program D cleared because it must pay the station 60 and its revenues will only increase by 55. On the other hand, it is in the interest of both parties to have program C cleared since otherwise network revenues will fall by 55, while the affiliate would have been willing to clear the program for a payment of only 50.

The critical point is that the clearance of A, B, and C maximizes the combined profits of the network and affiliate. That is, the total profits available to be divided between network and affiliate are largest when the affiliate carries this set of network programs. In principle, therefore, network and affiliate should be able to arrange a division of these profits that

Table 5.2 Illustration of the Determinants of Network Program Clearances

(1) Network programs	(2) Net revenue from nonnetwork program	(3) Value of Adjacencies	(4) Affiliate's reservation price (Col. 2 − Col. 3)	(5) Net revenue collected by Network	(6) Net revenue of network and affiliate from network program (Col. 3 + Col. 5)
A	100	70	30	55	125
B	95	55	40	55	110
C	90	40	50	55	95
D	85	25	60	55	80

makes both parties better off than if the affiliate carries any other collection of network programs.

Column 3 of table 5.2 shows the value of each time period when the nonnetwork alternative is broadcast, and column 6 reflects the combined net revenue of network and affiliate when the network program is carried. Column 6 combines the advertising revenue collected by the network as well as income to the affiliate from selling adjacencies. For A, B, and C the network programs add more to combined revenues than do nonnetwork programs. The clearance of program D would reduce combined revenue, however, because it adds 80 (55 to network revenue and 25 in revenue from adjacencies) to the combined revenues while the nonnetwork alternative generates a net revenue of 85.

The Economics of Profit Distribution:
Effects on Program Clearance

Clearly, networks and their affiliates have considerable incentive to maximize joint profits. But program clearance is not the only issue upon with these firms must agree. Some method must be devised to divide the resulting joint profits between a network and its affiliates.

To some extent, the division of profits will depend on differences in bargaining power between a network and its affiliate. For example, suppose two VHF stations are identically situated except that station x exists in a market with three other VHF stations and station y is in a market with only two other VHF stations. We would expect that the network would enjoy more power in bargaining with station x than with station y. In fact, our empirical tests reveal that stations like y do receive significantly higher network compensation rates than do stations like x.[6]

Such differences in bargaining power do not, however, affect the parties' incentive to clear the number and type of programs that maximize joint profits. Nevertheless, other factors may lead the parties to clearance decisions that fail to achieve this goal.

The following section provides an economic analysis of how the manner in which these profits are distributed may in fact affect clearance decisions and consequently prevent joint profits from being as large as possible. Note that this phenomenon cannot arise where the network and the station are owned by the same firm. In such cases, the firm has every reason to maximize joint profits from the twin activities of networking and broadcasting, and should be indifferent as to how these profits are allocated between these functions.

The Role of the Standard Compensation Plan: Separating
Clearance Decisions from Profit Distribution Decisions

Where the network and its affiliates are separate firms, the standard
compensation plan employed by the dominant networks provides a way to
separate the decision concerning how many programs to clear, and thus how
large the joint profits of network and affiliate will be, from the decision
concerning how they will divide those profits. Each network's affiliation
contract specifies a compensation rate for each daypart, and all programs
cleared within each daypart generate the same compensation. That flat
compensation rate must be at least equal to the highest reservation price the
station attaches to any program that is within the mix of programs the station
must clear to maximize joint profits. Yet, if the network pays that rate for all
programs cleared, the affiliate receives more than the sum of its reservation
prices for all programs within the desired mix. To illustrate this point,
assume, for example, that the numbers in table 5.2 reflect the situation of a
typical network and affiliate during prime time. In order to have programs
A, B, and C cleared, which would maximize joint profits, the station must
receive compensation of at least 50 per program. If the network offers
compensation of 50 on all programs cleared, however, the station will
receive more than its reservation price on A and B. For example, the station
would clear A for a payment of only 30 and B for only 40, a total of 70. With
compensation set at 50, it receives a payment for A and B of 100, or 30 more
than is required to induce their clearance.

The economic function of deductions is to provide a way to "return" to
the network some of these "extra" profits earned on A and B without
affecting affiliates' clearance behavior.[7] For example, if the station receives
50 for each additional hour cleared but an amount equal to 30 is deducted
from total compensation, regardless of the number of clearances, the outcome is the same as if the network had paid as compensation the reservation
price for each program. Deductions could not be set higher than 30 since the
station could earn higher profits from discontinuing its affiliation. These
deductions could, however, be lower than 30 if the station has some bargaining power. The exact level at which deductions will be set, then, will be
determined by the relative bargaining position of the two parties. We found,
for example, that deductions are often reduced or eliminated for VHF
affiliates in markets where at least one of the other affiliates operates on
UHF.[8] Presumably, this results from the superior bargaining power of these
VHF stations, which is in turn due to their technical superiority over UHF
outlets.

Factors Preventing Clearances That Maximize Joint Profits

No system of deductions, however, can be completely effective in separating clearance decisions from issues of profit division where the network does not own the stations. Strategic bargaining, transactions costs, the possibility of new network entry, and FCC regulations may serve to prevent simple joint profit maximization.

The Strategic Use of Information

Maximization of joint profits requires than at least one party have access to all available information regarding the value of each network program and its nonnetwork alternative. Either party (or both), however, may decide not to divulge information unavailable to the other in order to improve its position in bargaining over the division of profits. The affiliate, for example, may overstate its net revenues from nonnetwork programming in order to obtain higher network compensation. Similarly, the network may understate the amount it can pay in order to lower compensation levels.[9]

One possible strategy for a station is to refuse to clear a network program, even though clearance would increase joint profits, in order to induce the network to pay higher compensation in the future. In addition, a network may offer less than the maximum compensation it is willing to pay in the hope that the amount will still be sufficient to induce the affiliate to clear. In both cases, the effect may be that there are fewer clearances than the amount that would maximize joint profits of network and stations.[10]

Transactions Costs

Transactions costs render it uneconomical for the network to negotiate compensation with each affiliate for each network program. Consequently, network-affiliate contracts specify simple formulas by which compensation is determined for a small number of program periods. Since these are negotiated on the basis of the expected profitability of network and nonnetwork programs within each daypart, they do not take account of special situations that occur after the contracts have been signed. Thus, for example, an affiliate may choose not to clear a network program that develops relatively low rating although the network would be willing and able to pay the higher compensation required to obtain clearance. The problem arises when the high costs of negotiating special compensation for such a program outweigh the advantages of having the program cleared.[11]

The Possibility of New Network Entry

The analysis to this point has proceeded on the assumption that the existing structure of the broadcasting industry (the number of networks and the number of stations) is given. Within this structure, the interests of network and affiliate diverge only with respect to the distribution of joint profits between them. Therefore, if the preemption of a network program produces larger joint profits than does its clearance, both network and station can benefit if the nonnetwork program is carried. In that case, because network compensation would have to exceed the value to the network of the clearance in order for the program to be carried, the network would not attempt to have it cleared.

There is, however, an alternative. The network (and its affiliates) might be willing to forego some profits in the short run if such abstinence could prevent the entry of new program sources (or networks) over the long run. (We analyze this possibility and evaluate its likelihood in detail in the following chapter.) At this point, a brief example of the effects of a foreclosure strategy on clearance levels will suffice.

In the example presented above, the network paid compensation to the station sufficient only to have programs A, B, and C carried. Program D was not carried because the network could only obtain its clearance at a level of compensation that reduced overall profits. But suppose that, if the supplier of the alternative to program D could succeed in getting a large number of affiliates to carry its program, that supplier could then develop enough expertise and resources to become competitive with program C as well. That is, the alternative supplier's success in distributing program D would, over a period of time, enhance its ability to compete with the network during other time periods. If this were to occur, the profits of the network would eventually be reduced. The network therefore might pay the affiliate an amount large enough to induce the clearance of program D in order to prevent this long-run competitive threat.

As explained in the following chapter, we doubt that any such foreclosure strategy in fact underlies any of the affiliation contract provisions employed by the networks. If such a strategy were adopted, however, it would, as in the preceding example, require deviation from simple joint profit maximizing clearance patterns.

FCC Regulations

One Commission regulation, the Prime Time Access Rule, flatly forbids affiliates to clear certain amounts of most types of network prime-time programs. That rule obviously affects the parties' abilities to agree on program clearances that would maximize joint profits. Two other kinds of FCC regulations work to affect the clearance decision, but their combined effects are more indirect. These regulations are the Commission's group ownership rule, which requires that most local outlets for network programs be owned by entities other than the network, and the panoply of rules, largely derived from the Chain Broadcasting Rules, that limit the kinds of terms the parties may agree upon in bargaining over clearances.

The group ownership rule. We have already noted two reasons why the group ownership rule may reduce the joint profits of the network and the station. The separate ownership of station and network may increase the cost of transactions compared with the case of common ownership. Further, separate ownership means that the network and the station are likely, at least occasionally, to engage in strategic behavior in order to increase their respective shares of joint profits, with the result that some jointly profitable network programs may not be cleared.

If the preceding reasoning is correct, we should observe higher clearance rates for network programs by network-owned stations than by independent affiliates. Such an observation would confirm that one effect of the limitation of the number of stations that a network may own is to reduce the overall rate of network program clearances. Indeed, our study reveals that the clearance rate of network programs by network-owned stations is about 3 percentage points higher than that of affiliates during prime time (.98 to .95), an an even larger difference (.96 to .79), exists in other dayparts. Moreover, significant differences in clearance rates appear even when we control for other factors such as the size of the station's market and the number of competing stations.[12]

Regulation of the network-affiliate contract. It should be noted that the networks are likely to seek to accomplish through contracts with their affiliates what could otherwise be achieved more easily through ownership. Because the Commission regulates extensively the terms of network-affiliate contracts, however, observed differences in clearance rates between network-owned and independent stations may be due wholly or in part to the effects of these FCC rules and not solely to the group ownership limits. That is, the clearance behavior of affiliated and network-owned stations might be more similar, or even identical, if the chain broadcasting rules did not exist.

Accordingly, the role of FCC regulation is crucial to understanding the economics of the network-affiliate relationship. We need to know how the prohibited practices affect the clearance process and whether the introduction of regulation actually changed behavior or simply forced the parties to employ different means to achieve the same ends.

Although each regulation of the clearance agreement can be analyzed individually, general conclusions about their effects emerge from examining only a few. Here we trace the interrelated effects of the ban on option time and the restriction on graduated compensation plans.

Option time contract provisions required an affiliate to clear all network programs offered by the network during certain parts of the broadcast day called "option periods." In effect, the station agreed to take a "package" of network programs and, during the option periods, had only a limited right to decide whether or not to carry a given network program.

The effect of banning option time can be analyzed by considering the situation of the hypothetical affiliate depicted in table 5.2. If option time provisions were permitted, the affiliate might agree to option its time periods for programs A, B, and C in return for compensation of at least 40 per program. Total compensation for all programs (120) would thus equal the combined reservation prices for each program (30 + 40 + 50), and the collection of network programs that maximizes joint profits would be carried. In effect, the network and the station would have agreed, in a single transaction, on both the total amount of compensation and the amount of network programming to be carried. The device does more than simply reduce transactions cost. Option time provisions also limit the ability of affiliates to use strategic behavior to obtain a larger share of joint profits, since the affiliate must agree to both compensation and clearance levels at the time the affiliation agreement is negotiated.

The effect of the ban on option time depends, among other things, upon whether an alternative arrangement can be found for achieving the objectives sought through the use of option time. If, for example, there were no restrictions on the nature of compensation plans, the network could offer the affiliate 50 per program cleared, which would induce it to clear programs A, B, and C, and could deduct an amount up to 30 from total compensation. Thus, the same number of programs would be cleared and the same distribution of profits between network and affiliate could be accomplished as could be achieved through the use of option time.

A ban on option time therefore encourages the use of a graduated compensation plan since, in effect, the station is receiving nothing for the clearance of program A and a total of 120 for the clearance of B and C. The graduated compensation method does not fully substitute for option time, however, because, without option time, the station can obtain affiliation without agreeing on the level of clearances and hence is in a position to withhold clearance of some programs (or threaten to do so) in an effort to raise network compensation levels on all programs.

Suppose, now, that the Commission requires that the same compensation be paid for each network program cleared and further forbids the networks to contract for deductions from compensation. Examining the hypothetical station described in table 5.2, the effect of this restriction is that only programs A and B will be cleared. To obtain clearance for program A alone, the network would have to pay compensation of 30, which leaves it with profits of 25—the difference between the network's advertising receipts, 55, and the compensation payment. To get both A and B cleared, compensation of 40 per program must be paid, and the network would obtain 30 as the difference between its receipts from A and B of 110 and the compensation payment of 80. Since this amount exceeds the profit the network obtains when only A is cleared, it will be in the interest of the network to offer compensation of at least 40. However, it will be less profitable for the network to offer 50 per program, the amount required to have A, B, and C cleared. Although network advertising revenue would rise to 165, its compensation payments would increase to 150, leaving the network a total profit of only 15. Clearly, if the same amount of compensation must be paid for all programs, the network would be better off if only A and B were to be cleared.[13]

As noted earlier, however, combined profits are maximized when A, B, and C are carried. Consequently, the combined effect of a ban on option time and a complete prohibition of all graduated compensation plans would be to reduce joint profits and the clearance of network programs. It might also result in a shift of profits from networks to stations.[14]

Of course, the Commission has not completely prohibited graduated compensation plans, so permissible forms of graduation are already available for evading some of the effects of the prohibition on option time. Equally important, other techniques also are available for partially circumventing a ban on option time or graduated compensation plans. One involves the redefinition of dayparts. If for example, A, B, and C can be reclassified into different dayparts and the network sets compensation at 30, 40, and 50 respectively for the three dayparts, then the effect would be the same as under the graduated compensation scheme. Yet, although the

Commission has acted to reduce the extent to which network compensation plans can include graduated payments, the Commission has never expressed concern with variations in compensation among dayparts.

Yet another possible variation in compensation arrangements the networks could employ to obtain additional clearances would be to alter the mix of advertising time between network and station. A network faced with a prohibition against highly graduated compensation plans might, for example, pay similar amounts of direct compensation for the clearance of all network programs but make available to stations a larger proportion of advertising time for those programs that the network believes affiliates might not otherwise clear. In so doing, the network could obtain a high clearance rate without using a highly graduated compensation plan. The Commission has not addressed this possibility.

The network encounters a disadvantage, however, in seeking clearances in this manner. In the absence of a need to vary advertising time to achieve clearances, the network would choose that mix of network and station advertising time that would maximize net revenues from advertising sales. Station compensation would then be used to effect the clearance of programs, and deductions from compensation would assist in distributing profits between network and station. If the mix of advertising time is employed to induce clearance of programs, however, it cannot simultaneously be used to maximize net advertising revenues, since the mix that encourages any given number of programs to be cleared will not, in general, maximize those revenues. The utility of varying the mix of advertising time to encourage clearances is thus limited by the effect on net revenues of changes in that mix.[15]

These adaptations in response to Commission regulation do not, of course, exhaust all of the possibilities. But while one could expand the list, which would inevitably be incomplete, the basic points have already been made. So long as the incentives of network and affiliate are unchanged, attempts will be made to evade the effects of regulation. Moreover, the actions taken to evade regulation are likely to be difficult to observe and to separate from other alterations that occur as a result of changes in external economic forces. Finally, the evasion will usually be incomplete. As long as the regulations are at least partially effective, however, their effect will be to reduce the number of network programs cleared below the joint profit maximizing amount. These policies may also result in a redistribution of profits from networks to affiliates.

Conclusions

The fundamental economics of the network-affiliate relationship are complex indeed, but this complexity should not obscure certain fundamental, easily understood facts. Just as television networks arise in order to supply programs economically to geographically dispersed local outlets, so the relationship between networks and their affiliates is dominated by the questions of what network programs the affiliate will carry and at what gain to each party.

When one considers the incentives of networks and their affiliates, and the options available to both, the principal conclusion is that both parties have a great incentive to maximize the joint profits that accrue from networking and broadcasting. In most material respects, then, these entities are partners, not adversaries. Networks will not, except in isolated and extreme cases, be able to induce affiliates to clear programs not profitable for affiliates; indeed, except in equally isolated and extreme cases, the network would have no reason to do so if it could. These principles apply whether or not the same firm owns the network and the affiliate.

Where joint ownership does not exist, certain circumstances may arise in which the parties' incentives to maximize joint profits are not fully realized. Strategic bargaining over the distribution of profits may produce clearance levels that fail to maximize joint profits in the short run. Transactions costs may prevent the parties from adjusting to unanticipated events as quickly as they might otherwise wish to do. Present FCC regulations of clearance agreements may make joint profit maximization difficult or expensive, although such regulations are likely to lead the parties to adopt other techniques in an attempt to achieve their shared goals.

Volumes of analysis of network economic behavior, by the Commission and by independent researchers, have often seemed filled with fears or assertions that networks plunder affiliates' profits, force them to exhibit unprofitable or unpalatable fare, or prevent them from participating in programming decisions. At first blush, such assertions seem quite incredible; they appear utterly oblivious to the economic system in which the parties in fact cooperate.

Looked at more carefully, such claims probably often stem from a failure to distinguish the parties' shared interests in maximizing their joint profits and their divergent incentives in dividing those profits. Relatively marginal disputes concerning the division of profits are likely to be more visible to the public than the underlying implicit agreement on joint profit maximization, even though this congruence of interests pervades the relationship and, in fact, largely determines the fare offered to viewers.

At the very least, those who advance such fears or assertions would do well to realize that the principal "benefit" of policies, such as a ban on option time, that resolve these disputes externally is likely to be a reallocation of profits from network to affiliate, not any change in the value viewers derive from television. More careful attention should be paid to the question whether any public interest is served by governmental resolution of such disputes. To answer that question requires that we view FCC network-affiliate regulations through the optic of the economics of that relationship and measure them against the criteria developed earlier.

6   Evaluation of Network-Affiliate Regulations

This chapter assesses the role of regulation as it affects the formal and informal relationships between commercial television networks and their affiliates. We analyze both existing and proposed regulations, and attempt, in the conclusion, to describe a policy toward regulation of the network-affiliate relationship that is superior to those adopted or advanced to date.

Principal Existing Regulations

The relatively large number of FCC rules and regulations concerning network relationships with broadcast stations address four separate concerns. One group is directed at restraints networks may impose on their affiliates' program choices. These regulations govern the term of affiliation agreements, protect the affiliate's right to reject network programs, and prohibit exclusive affiliation agreements, option time and highly graduated compensation plans. Another group results from fears that the networks and their affiliates may behave anticompetitively in the advertising market. These rules prevent networks from controlling their affiliates' national spot rates or representing their affiliates in the national spot market. A third concern, that affiliates may disadvantage other stations by their arrangments with networks, underlies the rule forbidding affiliates to obtain territorial exclusivity from their networks. Finally, the one-affiliation-per-station rule results from a number of concerns over network practices in selecting affiliates.

We address each of these four regulatory concerns in turn. In each case we attempt to employ the preceding economic analysis to assess the extent to which these regulations help to attain the goals we have asserted should underlie governmental regulation of network structure and performance.

Restraints on Affiliates' Program Choices

Our analysis of the economics of the network-affiliate relationship examined in detail the effects of option time provisions and graduated compensation plans. We concluded that these provisions are likely to affect principally the division of profits between networks and their affiliates, but may also influence the number of network programs cleared, the transactions costs of networking, and the conditions of entry confronting potential new networks. Rules that limit the duration of affiliation contracts, prohibit affiliates from relinquishing a right to reject network programs, and ban exclusive affiliation agreements will produce the same effects, for the same reasons offered with respect to option time and graduated compensation.

None of these regulations may be said to prevent networks from inducing affiliates to take unprofitable programs, because the networks have no power or incentive to do so in the absence of such rules. All these rules make it more difficult for the networks to employ contract terms to simulate ownership of affiliates. Consequently, by providing affiliates and networks with additional opportunities to engage in strategic bargaining over the distribution of profits, all make it more expensive, and thus more difficult, to arrive at levels of program clearance that maximize the joint profits of network and affiliate. The rules may also make it somewhat more costly for networks and their affiliates to deter entry by potential new networks.

The rules should be evaluated by assessing the extent to which each of their possible effects is likely to occur and whether those results further defensible regulatory goals. Our analysis of the criteria by which network regulations should be judged provides the starting point. For the reasons set forth in that analysis, to the extent that the rules alter the distribution of profits between networks and affiliates or reduce the number of network programs cleared, they serve no discernible public purpose. Insofar as the rules prevent the dominant, conventional networks from deterring entry by new networks, they further the goal of stimulating competition. If, however, the rules simply increase the costs of networking, they frustrate attainment of that goal by hindering some, but not all, networks from providing service at the lowest possible cost.

For several reasons, we believe these rules, judged by our criteria, do not stand up under close scrutiny. First, it is more likely that the forbidden practices, if engaged in by the networks, would be adopted to reduce costs rather than to deter entry. Second, if an entry deterrence strategy would prove successful, these rules would be unlikely to prevent its adoption; other rules would stand a much better chance of success. Third, extending these rules to encompass all networks would be at best an expensive undertaking, at worst counterproductive to the goal of fostering competition. Finally, by any analysis, these rules do nothing to affect network dominance directly and so waste regulatory resources that could otherwise be employed to foster competition, enhance diversity, and increase localism.

Central to these conclusions is the proposition that the rules prohibit practices that are likely to reduce the costs of networking but are unlikely to affect network entry barriers. Accordingly, we review each of these alternatives at the outset.

Cost Reduction

We have observed that the network-affiliate relationship exhibits characteristics of both cooperation and rivalry. A network and its affiliates act cooperatively because both have an incentive to maximize the total profits from network programs, given the affiliates' nonnetwork program alternatives. Whether or not the network owns all its affiliates, this incentive to maximize joint profits will dominate program clearance decisions.

When the network does not own its affiliates, however, network-affiliate rivalry will emerge at a second decision-making stage, the division of profits between the two parties. Although each party has an incentive to maximize the total amount of profits to be divided between them, each also has an incentive to obtain the largest possible share of those profits. This, in turn, can lead to what we have called the strategic use of information.

Many of these barriers to joint profit maximization result from the fact that the network and its affiliates are generally owned by two separate entities and consequently may be expected to differ on how the profits should be divided between them. By contractually constraining the program choices of its affiliates, and thereby simulating network ownership of each affiliate, the network can limit the ability of its affiliate to engage in strategic behavior.

Thus the types of contract provisions forbidden by this panoply of existing regulations could have two distinct effects in reducing the costs of networking. First, by reducing the opportunity for strategic bargaining by affiliates, use of these contract provisions would better enable the network to produce a program schedule that maximizes the combined income of network and affiliates. Second, many of these practices would reduce the number (and therefore the costs) of separate network-affiliate transactions that must be concluded in order to permit exhibition of that joint profit-maximizing schedule.

In a sense, of course, this conclusion is tautological. Networks would adopt these presently forbidden practices only to increase profits or to reduce costs. The point, however, is that adoption of those practices is quite likely to signal the realization of lower costs, unless some anticompetitive gain may be realized as well.

Entry Deterrence

At first blush, it may appear equally likely that networks would employ these practices to inhibit the entry of new networks. Most of the practices reviewed here—lengthy or exclusive affiliation agreements, option time, and provisions denying affiliates the right to reject network programs—will have the apparent effect, when invoked, of preventing or hindering affiliates from presenting programs other than those offered by the contracting network. Further, highly graduated compensation plans appear to reserve high network payments for programs otherwise not likely to be cleared. Therefore, all these practices might tie up existing broadcast outlets, denying or inhibiting access to them by additional networks.

Reflection suggests, however, that these kinds of provisions are ill-designed for purposes of entry deterrence. There are probably less cumbersome means available to networks seeking to erect entry barriers; certainly regulatory measures are available to combat such a strategy without risking interference with network-affiliate bargaining tactics. These conclusions rest in part upon the kind of entry deterrence that regulators should discourage.

What kind of entry matters?

The practice that regulatory policy should guard against is deterrence of entry by additional full-scale networks. Two other kinds of entry could, but should not, occupy regulators' attention. First, a new network may merely displace an existing network, leaving the total number of networks unchanged. Such "entry" does little or nothing to further any of the goals of regulation described above, for it simply changes the name of the firm operating the network.[1] In any event, prohibition of the affiliation practices under review here would do nothing to further the prospects of such displacement-entry. If a new full-time network is potentially more profitable than an incumbent network, and the number of broadcast outlets is so limited that an additional network would not be profitable, then either the incumbent network will purchase the new network's programs or the new network will purchase the affiliation rights of the incumbent or, more likely, simply purchase the incumbent entirely. In neither event would the incumbent gain an additional advantage from provisions in its affiliation contract.

A second type of "new" network might be a part-time network that would displace an incumbent, but only during time periods in which the emergent network's programming was more profitable than the incumbent's. Some might fear that without regulation the incumbent's restraints on affiliates' program choices (e.g., exclusive affiliation) would be used to deter such entry. In fact, however, since full-time networks enjoy substantial economies of scale, the new and the established networks would find it mutually profitable for the incumbent to buy the newcomer's programs or for the latter to acquire and operate the former. For the incumbent, deterring entry is a less profitable policy than merger.

Even if this prediction is erroneous, partial displacement of an established full-time network by a new part-time network would do little to further the goals of network regulation discussed above. After such "entry," at any one time viewers could receive only the same number of networks, over the same number of television outlets, as before. Thus neither competition for viewers nor diversity nor localism, as we would measure those values, is promoted by a rule facilitating part-time displacement of a full-time network, even if such displacement could occur in the face of the economies realized by full-time networks.

Network program restraints on affiliates and conditions of entry into networking. Restraints on affiliates' program choices imposed in network-affiliate contracts should be treated as undesirable by federal policy, then, only if those restraints affect the conditions of entry confronting additional full-scale networks. Those restraints presently prohibited by FCC regulation cannot have such an effect, however, unless the existing three networks extract these contractual provisions not simply from three affiliates in each market, but also from at least one other station in several key markets. Restrictive affiliation agreements between each network and only a single affiliate in each market would leave any unaffiliated stations as potential affiliates of a new network. Consequently, so long as each network has only one affiliate in each market, the regulated contractual practices cannot be viewed as devices for foreclosure. It is only when these practices are extended to "second" affiliates that they might conceivably raise the specter of foreclosure or entry deterrence.

This is not to deny that incumbent networks have the incentive to adopt affiliation practices that may deter entry by additional networks. Indeed, quite the converse may well be true.

Existing networks may realize gains from deterring entry for two reasons. First, the addition of new networks may reduce the prices that each network obtains from advertising sales, by fragmenting viewing audiences, increasing competition in the advertising market, or both. Second, the new network may increase competition for programming so that the share of program revenues acquired by the producers of programs and their associated talent increases. Consequently, both existing networks and their affiliates may have an interest in policies that inhibit the formation of new networks.

Whether a strategy for deterring entry is profitable depends upon whether the aggregate profits of the incumbent networks following implementation of such a strategy are greater than the aggregate profits of the incumbents and the new network if entry occurs. Aggregate network revenues may well be increased by forestalling entry because new network entry will not be likely to expand total viewing sufficiently to offset its effect on advertising rates and program costs.

A deterrence strategy could succeed, however, only if multiple affiliations in individual markets were permitted. Further, an examination of the economics of such tactics suggests that the venture would be frangible, at best. To illustrate the latter point requires some elaboration of the necessary collective choices that the existing dominant networks would have to make to erect an effective entry barrier to a fourth rival.

If network ownership of stations were not regulated, the three networks could acquire a sufficient number of broadcast outlets in sufficient key markets and then refuse to sell these stations' services to a fourth network.[2] Each incumbent network could decide to operate only one station in each market if programming the "excess" stations would lower profits. Alternatively, if fear of governmental intervention mandated that the "excess" stations carry some programs, each (or one) of the networks might form a "dual" network composed of these stations and exhibit on that network very inexpensive programming.[3]

In the presence of the Commission's ownership rules, however, an entry-deterrence strategy would have to be implemented by the networks' securing multiple affiliations in enough key markets and employing those affiliation practices (exclusive affiliation, option time, etc.) that simulate affiliate ownership. If permitted, such a strategy could have the effect of inhibiting network entry, but we doubt that tactic could be implemented.

First, to prevent entry by additional full-scale networks, existing networks would have to secure multiple affiliations in many markets and pay owners of otherwise independent stations an amount at least equal to that which they could earn through affiliation with a new network.[4] If a ban on dual networking were absent, the networks could provide their "second" affiliates with very inexpensive programs. In the presence of a ban (or a fear that merely duplicating existing networks' programs would lead to governmental intervention), the "second" affiliates would clear none of the incumbent networks' programs and continue to program as independents. These independents, however, would receive payments from the incumbent networks (equal to the difference in profits earned from affiliating with a new network and those earned as an independent) for refusing to affiliate with a new network. Therefore, whichever programming technique the incumbent networks adopted, much of the gain from deterring entry would be "captured" by the potential affiliates of the new network rather than by the incumbent networks. Indeed, the amount that would have to be paid might exceed the increase in the profits of the incumbents.

Existing networks would confront additional problems in implementing this deterrence strategy. First, they would have to agree among themselves on dividing the costs of the "bribe" to the potential affiliates.[5] Second, the original network affiliates can always threaten to breach or refuse to renew their contract if the profits from affiliation with the new network prove to be greater than those generated by their current affiliation agreements. To retain these affiliates, the existing networks would have to increase the share of network profits paid to affiliates. In short, not only would incumbents have to bribe their second affiliates not to affiliate with a new network, they might have to bribe their original affiliates as well.[6] In an extreme case, the original and secondary affiliates together could capture all of the profits from networking.

If the incumbent networks sought to deter a new entrant which either intended to be solely a part-time network or wished to start small and grow over time into a full-scale network, the foregoing analysis would be altered very little, The networks would still have to pay the additional value of the new network affiliation to existing independent stations, confront the difficulties of how the cost of such a bribe would be divided among the incumbent networks, and face demands for additional compensation that might arise from their original affiliates.

Cost Reduction vs. Entry Deterrence

One cannot conclude with complete assurance that an entry-deterring strategy will not in fact be practiced by the incumbent networks. It is highly probable, however, that such a strategy would be difficult to implement and would hold out the prospect of little or no gain to the incumbents.

In these circumstances, the particular regulations under discussion here should not be defended on the grounds that banning these affiliation practices will preclude strategic entry deterrence by the networks. Certainly none of these contractual practices is necessarily designed to prevent new entry. Indeed, persuasive arguments suggest that they reduce the costs to networks of ensuring that affiliates will clear the profit-maximizing number of programs. Most importantly, these practices become suspect only when applied by a network to more than one affiliate in each of several markets. To preclude new network entry, it is not sufficient that these practices apply to only one affiliate per market: the incumbent networks must also be able to deny access by a new network to enough potential affiliates of the new entrant.

The dual networking and ownership rules may have impeded the ability of the incumbent networks to preclude new entry. Notwithstanding these rules, the incumbent networks might still succeed in preventing entry through multiple affiliations within key markets, although we believe such a strategy is more likely to enrich affiliates than their networks. More importantly, any foreclosure that did occur would not stem from the specific provisions in affiliation contracts at issue here, but rather from the simple fact of multiple affiliations with stations in several individual markets.

Finally, entry deterrence is a plausible goal only if a fourth full-time advertiser-supported network is viable. In fact, the possibility of a fourth such over-the-air network was virtually nil from 1956 to 1976, and is still probably not very great.[7] This suggests that the networks did not implement the practices of option time and highly graduated compensation plans for the purpose of preventing new network entry. In effect, because the possibility that an additional full-time advertiser-supported over-the-air television network could come into existence has been so remote, there have been no potential network entrants to deter.

Alternatives Confronting the Commission

For all these reasons, the congeries of FCC regulations governing those terms of network affiliation contracts that structure program clearance decisions should be evaluated in two ways. First, their principal effects—to alter the distribution of income between networks and their affiliates or to reduce the number of network programs cleared—serve no defensible public purpose. Second, they have the additional effect of preventing agreement on terms that, if implemented, would reduce the costs of networking.

On these bases alone the regulations seem undesirable. But the regulations no longer exist in the sheltered environment of a three-network system. The alternatives actually confronting the Commission include not only removing or retaining these regulations, but also extending them to new network forms or redefining the types of networks subject to their proscriptions. Careful consideration of these alternatives suggests that, with one important qualification, the more relevant question is not whether, but when, the Commission will repeal these regulations.

Coverage of the present rules. As previously noted, this group of rules applies to any nascent network with two or more electronically interconnected conventional broadcast station affiliates. The rules do not apply to program distribution methods that do not employ simultaneous interconnection or that rely solely on cable or MDS affiliates. Nor do the rules apply to nonbroadcast station affiliates even if the program distributor's "network" consists in part of (at least two) conventional broadcast outlets. Where such a network configuration exists, the rules apply only to affiliation contracts with those conventional outlets.

Why extended coverage is indefensible. The Commission must consider, given the expansion of network forms, whether an extension of the rules to all new network forms would further its policy goals. The answer appears to be no. As the FCC itself has concluded in the case of radio networks, the very appearance of new networks and additional broadcast outlets, regardless of the technology employed, mitigates the concerns expressed by the Commission in the promulgation of these rules. As new networks and new broadcast outlets appear, the extent of competition among networks for affiliates may increase, and there will be increased possibility that new and diverse sources of programming will be broadcast, and individual broadcast outlets will have a greater array of program choices confronting them. In these circumstances, the practices presently prohibited could not conceivably be employed to avoid further network entry, in the absence of separately remediable overt agreements among this wider number of rival networks.

Moreover, an extension of the rules may actually have the perverse effect of impeding new network entry, without providing any countervailing advantages to competition, diversity, or localism. We observed that the contractual constraints stipulated by the rules may reduce networking costs by reducing the extent of strategic misrepresentation on the part of affiliates. If new networks are prohibited from adopting contractual practices that maximize their profits, the number of new networks might be less than it would be otherwise. Certainly this is the conclusion reached by the Commission in 1977 when, in repealing these rules as applied to radio, it concluded that some of them might deter new or innovative radio networks.[8] For all these reasons, one is hard put even to conjecture a plausible basis for extending these rules to new network forms.

Cable networks, however, may require special consideration. In the recent past, cable systems in some cases promised distributors of pay programming that the cable system would not exhibit the pay programming of any other distributor during the lifetime of the contract. Such agreements differ substantially from exclusivity arrangements between conventional networks and their broadcast station affiliates because conventional network arrangements affect only one local broadcast channel whereas a cable exclusivity agreement affects several local channels. The difference in part stems from the fact that each conventional broadcast channel in any particular market is owned by a different entity while a single entity owns all the cable channels. No desire for efficiency can justify such all-encompassing cable exclusivity provisions and, although it may be doubted whether such agreements are designed to confer on the pay programmer local monopoly power, it seems clear that they can retard the development and growth of new pay cable networks. Put simply, such agreements deny viewers additional programming options.

Note that the analysis here is formally identical to that of the network's use of multiple affiliation in a single market designed to prevent the birth of an additional network. The pay-cable network in effect affiliates itself with all the channels of a cable system that would otherwise be devoted to additional pay programmers. For the same reasons as in the network case, we would expect the cable operator to capture a large share of the gains from such entry exclusion. We would also, therefore, expect this tactic to be equally unlikely to succeed. Indeed, exclusivity is no longer a general practice. Cable systems now often carry pay programming services provided by a number of different distributors.[9] Nevertheless, because there is usually only one cable operator in a franchise area, it is conceivable (particularly in small markets) that the cable operator (as opposed to the pay programmer) may wish to limit the number of pay program services it offers. Because such a practice could limit the options available to viewers, the Commission or Congress might find it desirable to adopt policies that ensure greater access by pay programmers to cable systems.[10]

Whether or not such a policy is desirable depends upon the availability of other outlets (e.g., direct broadcast satellites, multichannel MDS) for the local distribution of pay programming. Put simply, if competition exists among local video distribution services, there may be no reason for the adoption of such policies, notwithstanding the fact that typically there is only one cable system in any particular geographic area. Further, the reward to the cable operator from granting exclusivity is reduced if the programmers that are denied access to the cable system can employ alternative distribution systems. This makes an exclusivity strategy even more unlikely.

Why presently limited coverage is indefensible. A potential additional network subject to the Commission's present regulations of program clearance decisions confronts a regulatory-induced entry barrier in that its expected profits would be lower under these rules than without them. The entrant, however, might completely or partially escape the restrictions imposed by these rules simply by not affiliating with conventional over-the-air broadcasting stations. Thus a network that affiliated solely with MDS or cable outlets would be free to engage in the otherwise prohibited practices since it would not fall within the definition of a network under the chain broadcasting rules. Similarly, a new network that adopted a mixed affiliation pattern by affiliating partially with conventional broadcast stations and partially with unconventional outlets that are not "broadcast stations" subject to the rule, might be able to increase its anticipated profits beyond those it could expect to earn if all its affiliates were subject to the rules.[11]

Providing potential entrants an inducement to adopt such "biased" affiliation patterns would have at least three potential costs. First, despite the fact that the new network could earn greater profits by avoiding the rule, its profits would still be less than they would be without the rules, i.e., the rules would still impose a barrier to entry. Second, to the extent that the costs of a biased affiliation pattern exceed the costs of employing broadcast affiliates, the rules result in inefficiencies. Third, by providing an artificial inducement to bypass conventional broadcast outlets, the rules may adversely affect VHF and UHF stations that might otherwise secure a network affiliation.

Conclusions

Economic analysis of the network-affiliate relationship indicates that, as applied to the current three commercial networks, existing regulations of affiliation agreements terms addressed to program clearance decisions have failed to further the goals of competition, diversity, and localism. These failures, in turn, have resulted from a persistent inability or unwillingness to recognize that a network and its affiliates have a joint incentive to maximize the profitability of network operation. When this elementary concept is understood, it clearly emerges that the practices regulated by this group of rules were designed largely to minimize attempts by affiliates to capture a larger profit share. In addition, it is highly unlikely that the regulated contractual provisions were designed by the networks to forestall new network entry.

Maintaining the status quo with respect to these regulations not only fails to achieve any beneficial goals, but will produce several undesirable results. Their existence tends to bias affiliation choices away from over-the-air broadcast stations to outlets employing newer technologies, even if affiliation would otherwise be less costly with the former. By reducing the anticipated profitability of new networks, the rules may have the perverse effect of limiting the number of new networks that may be viable. In addition, some viewers could be denied additional options in those markets where cable or MDS systems have not penetrated simply because a new network may not find it profitable to affiiliate with broadcast stations as a result of the rules. Neither the goal of competition nor that of diversity is served by these results.

Although an extension of the rules to all new network forms would prevent these distortions, such a policy would reduce the profitability of new networks by compelling them to adopt more costly techniques for ensuring clearance of their programs. This, in turn, might reduce the number of viable networks without any compensating gains—a result hardly consistent with any identifiable policy objectives.

In any event, the very appearance of new networks and new broadcast outlets should substantially reduce the concerns that led the Commission to adopt the rules initially, as the Commission recognized when it repealed these rules with respect to radio networks. The goals of competition, localism, and diversity are all served by expanding the number of entities participating in the broadcast system and an appropriate regulatory policy is one that promotes such a result. Both maintaining the status quo and extending the coverage of the rules inhibit the attainment of these goals. As the number of rival television networks increases, then, the Commission will discover that these regulations concomitantly become increasingly indefensible. Unable to justify extending the rules, on the one hand, or applying them arbitrarily to "broadast" networks on the other, the FCC eventually will have no choice other than repeal.

A more substantial case can be made, however, for applying a prohibition on exclusive affiliation to firms, such as cable systems, that control several outlets in one market. For precisely the same reason, the number, rather than the types, of network affiliations within any one local market requires careful scrutiny. In both cases, the regulatory goal should be avoidance of market power within local viewing areas. Pursuing that policy would squarely target the problem, whereas present regulations address it only obliquely.

Restraints Imposed by the Networks on Their Affililates' Advertising Policies

Function of the Regulated Practices

The second group of rules regulating network-affiliate relationships prohibits networks from determining their affiliates' rates for the sale of non-network broadcast time and from representing their affiliates (other than their owned and operated stations) in the sale of national advertising time. Both rules may be defended on the grounds that they reduce the possibility of collusion in setting national advertising rates by prohibiting networks from controlling or influencing directly the rates of the closest substitutes for network advertising, national spot sales.

If each network could set the advertising rates of its affiliates, and all three networks also were able to collude tacitly or overtly on what those rates should be, the three networks could (by virtue of the difference between television advertising and other forms of advertising) wield some power in the advertising market.

At any particular time, in any event, the value of advertising on one network may differ from that on any other network by virtue of that network's overall ratings performance. Each network is distinguished from the others by its ability to develop and schedule successful programs and consequently enjoys some discretion in setting its advertising rates. Moreover, the closest substitutes for within-program spots on a particular network are adjacencies on the same network schedule. By determining the prices for network spots as well as their closest substitutes (national spots appearing in network adjacences), a network could reduce the scope of competition with its affiliates for the patronage of national advertisers and earn greater profits. Understood in this manner, attempts to determine both these prices constitute attempts to engage in horizontal price-fixing. Indeed, during the Chain Broadcasting study NBC offered this explanation for adopting these practices in radio networking.[12]

The practice whereby networks represented their affiliates in the sale of national advertising could be considered a similar—if somewhat less effective—method of reducing price competition between networks and their affiliates. While representing their affiliates to advertisers, the networks could suggest to their affiliates what the "correct" national spot rate should be.

But there may also be efficiencies in this practice that do not seem to be present in the first. Because networks sell advertising time to national advertisers, they have established contacts with the most advertisers that participate in the national spot market and, of course, possess extensive information about their own network programming. For these reasons, networks may be able to represent their affiliates in the national spot market at costs lower than those of independent station representative firms.

A third motive may also help to explain such representation. As noted in chapter 5, an affiliate may have an incentive to mislead the network with respect to the relative values of the affiliate's network and nonnetwork alternatives in order to convince the network to increase the affiliate's compensation payments. Therefore, a network may also desire to represent its affiliates in the national spot market in order to acquire more information about the value of network and nonnetwork programs to its affiliates. In this way, the network may be able to reduce the amount of misleading information it receives from its affiliates, thereby reducing the costs of networking and increasing the profits going to the network.

Of course, none of these possible motives excludes any other. All could occur simultaneously. Some evidence suggests, however, that spot prices would not increase if the rule banning network representation of affiliates were repealed. Each network represents all its owned-and-operated stations in the national spot market. Recent analysis of national spot contracts revealed that in those markets containing a network-owned-and-operated station, national advertising spot prices were not significantly different from those in other markets.[13] This result is consistent with any of three hypotheses: (1) that no market power effects attend this representation; (2) that the reduction in costs flowing from the arrangement is sufficiently great to offset any market power that is created; or (3) that the network and spot markets in fact constitute a single market. If this third hypothesis were true, the networks would determine advertising prices for the entire market and network-owned-and-operated stations, like other stations, would take these prices as given. In this case, we would not expect any relationship between the presence in a market of network-owned-and-operated stations and spot advertising prices.

Effects of the Existing Rules

The prohibition on network control of affiliates' national spot rates appears to serve the goal of increasing competition. Localism (aside from the fact that pricing decisions remain in the hands of affiliates) and diversity do not seem to be either furthered or frustrated by the rule.

With respect to the prohibition on representation, the assessment is more complex. On the one hand, banning networks from representing their affiliates in the advertising market appears procompetitive because it reduces the probability that such arrangements may be employed indirectly to affect affiliates' prices. On the other hand, the rule may lessen competition either by prohibiting lower-cost suppliers of "rep" services (i.e., networks) from competing in that market or by increasing the costs of networking. As with the first rule, neither localism nor diversity appears to be furthered or frustrated by the rule.

Assessment of the Present Rules

Scope. As with the set of network-affiliate regulations directed at program clearance terms, any program distributor affiliated with two or more electronically interconnected broadcast outlets is defined by these advertising rules as a network. Distributors that do not employ simultaneous interconnection or that affiliate only with cable or MDS systems escape the rules.

Thus the advertising rules, as presently constituted, also may affect the conditions of entry confronting potential new networks or bias affiliation patterns. Accordingly, to evaluate the future efficacy of the present rules requires that we consider options additional to simple retention or repeal. From these perspectives, the two rules appear quite different.

Control of national spot rates. The prohibition of network control of affiliates' national spot rates appears to serve directly the goal of increasing competition, without denying networks or affiliates any offsetting efficiency gains. Neither localism (aside from the fact that pricing decisions remain in the hands of affiliates) nor diversity seems to be furthered or frustrated by the rule. For these reasons, the goal of competition would be furthered by extending the ban on network control over station rates to include nonconventional network forms. Such an extension would also eliminate one potential source of affiliation bias.

Assuredly, however, as new networks arise that are wholly or partially supported by advertising revenues, network control of affiliate advertising rates will be less effective in promoting market power. If enough advertiser-supported networks enter the television system, whatever power to set advertising rates individual networks now possess will be reduced or eliminated. If the FCC were able to conclude that such a competitive network market has arisen, the rule could easily be discarded.

Representaion of affiliates. With respect to representation by networks of their affiliates in the national spot market, the issue is more problematic. If in fact, such arrangements are efficient, then retention or extension of the rule may frustrate the Commission's objectives of competition, localism, and diversity. Retention may deny networks covered by the rule an efficient method of organization and may bias affiliation patterns toward nonbroadcast outlets. Extension, however, may deprive new networks of the full efficiencies of networking, thus reducing their anticipated profitability and possibly limiting the number of new networks that arise. Although banning these arrangments may limit the scope of market power of existing networks, the longer-term costs of such a policy may be to reduce the number of viable networks.

Resolution of the issue thus requires close judgement. The Commission must choose whether to pursue the possible immediate effects of avoiding the danger of collusive behavior by extending the rule or the possible longer-term effects of avoiding distortions in affiliation patterns or inhibitions on further network entry by repealing it. The preferable course appears to be repeal, either immediately or after a modest increase in advertiser-supported networks. Even the potential for entry of new networks will reduce the power to set prices of all networks by increasing the alternatives available to advertisers. At the same time, repeal would allow new networks to take full advantage of any efficiencies that stem from representing affiliates. Consequently, although in the short term repeal may enhance the market power of some networks, the Commission's goals of competition, diversity, and localism would best be served in the long run by a repeal of this rule, because new network entry will reduce even further the possibility that representation of affiliates can be put to anticompetitive ends.

If, notwithstanding the preceding argument, extension is preferred, the Commission should—by analogy with the program supply rules—consider exempting small networks from the rules. In those instances in which a fledgling network is competing in the same advertising market as the larger networks, an exemption might appear justified on the grounds that even if the smaller network were to employ affiliate representation as a device to reduce competition with its affiliates, any impact on the advertising market would be insignificant.

Even this option, however, entails risk. Small networks catering to specialized audiences and specialized advertisers may enjoy a degree of monopoly power, but would elude easy identification. Thus a "small network" blanket exemption might create or tolerate pockets of market power.[14] Such a policy, however, is at least equally likely to increase the number of viewer options—and thus diversity—by removing the rule's inhibitions from small networks that may require these practices for their very existence and to promote individual localism by increasing the range of alternative programming sources available to individual broadcast outlets.

The Rule Prohibiting Territorial Exclusivity

Function of the Regulated Practice

In the absence of Commission regulation, a network affiliate may find either a syndicated or locally originated program more profitable to broadcast than the network offering and will preempt the network program to air the substitute. However, the profitability of that nonnetwork program might be enhanced by the practice of territorial exclusivity which would prevent the rejected network offering from appearing on another station in the market. As a result, the affiliate may be willing to induce the network (for example, by agreeing to a lower compensation rate) not to exhibit programs of that network on another station in the market. Thus a practice of territorial exclusivity would be designed principally to enhance the profitability of network affiliates and would undoubtedly be accompanied by arrangements making it profitable for networks as well.

As a result of this practice, viewers may be deprived of a program option that is more popular than some of the programs actually exhibited.[15] The rule is thus designed to promote diversity of sources and individual localism by preventing affiliates and networks from enhancing their profits at the expense of viewers. When the range of options available to networks and affiliates is examined, however, the extent to which these purposes are achieved is unclear.

The rule banning territorial exclusivity originated as one of the Chain Broadcasting Rules and was extended, without serious consideration, to television while that industry was still in its infancy. Thus one cannot know whether territorial exclusivity would have been practiced widely in television networking in the absence of the rule.

Nevertheless, territorial exclusivity can be a profitable strategy only under rather stringent conditions. First, the profits of the affiliate's substitute program must be greater than the joint profits of the network and affiliate from the affiliate's exhibition of the network program.[16] Our research reveals that preemptions during prime time amount on average to less than 5 percent of the network's offerings.[17] Thus it is likely that a right of territorial exclusivity would be invoked only rarely.

Secondly, the profitability of the substitute program with territorial exclusivity protection must at least be equal to the total profits generated by the simultaneous exhibition of the substitute program by the affiliate and of the network program by a different station in that market (i.e., without exclusivity). Only under these circumstances can the affiliate pay the network an amount high enough to induce the network not to exhibit its program on another station. This means that the affiliate would have to purchase not only the exhibition rights to the substitute program but those to the preempted network program as well. This second condition dictates that affiliates will purchase territorial exclusivity even less frequently than they will preempt programs.

Moreover, networks and their affiliates may be able to practice territorial exclusivity without an explicit contractual provision. If avoiding exhibition of a preempted network program is jointly profitable for a network and its affiliate, the network might agree to accept the exhibition of the program by the affiliate at a time other than the original broadcast and the affiliate might agree to accept lower compensation. Alternatively, the network could simply decline to offer the preempted program to other stations in the market or offer it on unattractive terms. In either event, viewers may be denied the option altogether, even without explicit provision for territorial exclusivity.

Assessment of the Rule

Several reasons counsel against an optimistic assessment of the ban on teritorial exclusivity. Given the relative ease of avoiding the intent of the rule, its impact might simply be to increase the costs of negotiating exclusivity. Without any explicit contractual clause detailing the conditions under which such exclusivity is granted, the parties will bargain over which programs deserve territorial exclusivity and which do not. Given this possibility, the costs of bargaining over the applicability of an implied exclusivity agreement may be greater than if an agreement were explicitly specified. But there is no *a priori* way to determine if this increase in costs is sufficient to make all such implicit agreements unprofitable.

Further, if exclusivity is being granted implicitly, it may be impossible to draft a rule that prohibits the practice without the Commission becoming involved in fine details of the implicit contractual relationships between networks and their affiliates. Given the low rate of preemptions, and the even smaller number of programs for which exclusivity would be jointly profitable for the networks and their affiliates, such detailed regulation probably would not be justified.

Nevertheless, the purpose of the rule is in accord with the objectives of diversity and localism. That the rule may only make it more costly for networks and affiliates jointly to thwart these purposes is no reason to discard it, particularly when no plausible goal is disserved by the ban.

If these arguments are persuasive, then the rule should be extended to new network forms. We can imagine no justification for retaining any affiliation bias that may be induced by the rule's present restricted scope. Admittedly, extension might reduce the profitability of new full-time networks, but increasing their profitability is no more permissible a goal than increasing the profitability of ABC or its affiliates. Rather, the true goals at stake here are diversity and localism.

The "One Affiliation per Station" Rule

Function of the Regulated Practice

In the absence of Commission regulation, the networks would compete among themselves for affiliations in a given market, the value of an affiliation with any particular station being determined in part by the coverage of the station and the technical comparability of all the stations in the market. Conceivably, in markets where one station labors under a particularly severe coverage and technical handicap (e.g., a market with two VHF stations and one UHF station), a network unable to obtain a primary affiliation with a VHF station might still find it more profitable to obtain a secondary affiliation with one of the VHF stations rather than to seek a primary affiliation with the UHF station. In such cases, the UHF station is likely to be offered only those network programs not cleared by either VHF station in the market.

Although the Commission's rule merely requires that the UHF station (in our example above) have an extensive right of first call on the third network's programs, the practical effect of the rule is to mandate primary affiliation by the third network with the UHF station in a market where that station has "reasonably comparable facilities" to those of the other stations in the market. The goal of the rule might well be to increase UHF profitability and therefore, arguably, to promote competition (through increasing the possibility of entry by a fourth network) as well as diversity and localism (by promoting an increase in the number of broadcast outlets).[18]

In theory, however, the network should be able to capture any increase in profits that the UHF station experiences as a result of primary affiliation. The network could do so by paying the UHF station very little compensation, or even charging the station for the right to carry the network's programs.

Nevertheless, this latter practice might invite FCC scrutiny and thus may not be a real option for the network. Moreover, even without compensation, the UHF station may experience an increase in profitability through an increase in the value of its adjacencies. In this fashion, the rule may have increased the profitability of existing UHF stations and may have transformed some two-station markets into three-station markets through the prospect of network affiliation with that third station.

Assessment of the Rule

The foregoing effects of the rule lend it a veneer of respectabilty. In fact, the restriction, more carefully viewed, is a paradigmatic example of misguided regulation. The rule achieves no measurable benefit to viewers and is so badly drafted that it now unintentionally serves principally to protect ABC, CBS, and NBC from competition.

At present, this rule applies only to full-scale, interconnected, over-the-air networks that wish to adopt a secondary affiliation with a broadcast station that is affiliated with ABC, CBS, or NBC. Thus, although new full-time networks can engage in primary affiliation practices with any local outlet, they cannot seek secondary affiliations with television broadcast stations affiliated with ABC, CBS, or NBC.

Consequently, the effect of the rule today is purely anticompetitive. It restricts competition for affiliation among networks and restricts the program choices of the most valued stations at the expense of increasing the program choices of the least-valued stations. A new network that, in the absence of the rule, would have found it more profitable to obtain a secondary affiliation with, for example, a VHF station than to negotiate a primary affiliation with a UHF station, would now have to affiliate with the latter. This in turn may reduce the profitability of new networks and thus the prospects for new network entry. Conversely, without the rule, a new network may find it profitable to affiliate with the UHF station. Under the rule, however, the UHF station becomes the primary affiliate of an existing network and, so long as that network is not displaced from the market, is unavailable for affiliation with a new network. Moreover, because of the handicaps UHF stations operate under, some viewers may be denied the opportunity to watch the most popular network programs. In short, the rule much more effectively deters entry than does any of the contract practices forbidden by the FCC's other regulations.

Because of the failure of the existing rule to achieve its goals, because of the very limited impact the rule has had, because the need to promote one form of broadcast outlet decreases in the face of the growth of other broadcast forms, and because the rule may actually retard new network growth, repeal of the rule would certainly not hinder the Commission's goals of competition, diversity, and localism. Indeed, repeal of the rule may increase the extent to which these goals are achieved by increasing competition among networks for affiliates and increasing the array of program choices available to broadcast outlets. Certainly there is no reason to retain the limited insulation from competition for affiliates' time that the rule presently affords ABC, CBS, and NBC.

Proposed Additional or
Alternative Regulations

As recently as 1977, the FCC expressed serious interest in promulgating additional regulations concerning three aspects of the network-affiliate relationship: the length of network schedules, the structure of network compensation plans, and network-affiliate previewing practices.[19] Our

analysis of the Commission's existing rules that impose restraints on affiliates' program choices explains why neither of the first two proposals is
sound. The previewing proposal involves somewhat different policy issues,
but reflection suggests that the FCC should not adopt it, either.

Expansion of Network Schedules

We consider separately, in chapter 8, whether the Prime Time Access
Rule which forbids affiliates from clearing network programs during certain
times, furthers important public policies. This rule requires separate analysis because its proponents assert that the rule cures a myriad of ills, including
some arising from network program procurement practices, which are unrelated to the length of network schedules.

A more straightforward measure, if the length of network schedules is the
concern, would be a rule limiting the number of programs (or hours of
programming) that networks may offer, leaving to network-affiliate bargaining the decision of which time periods, if any, networks will vacate. If
the goal is to prevent expansion by existing networks, which would inhibit
new network entry, a flat limit on network schedules is clearly superior to
the Prime Time Access Rule, for it would strike directly at the asserted harm
without introducing regulatory constraints that are superfluous to any concern with preemptive foreclosure.

A limit on network schedules is not necessarily inconsistent with the
public interest. Indeed, prohibiting a schedule expansion whose sole purpose and effect is to foreclose new networks would serve the interest of
competition and, perhaps, that of diversity. No rule, however, expressed in
terms of a maximum number of programs or hours, would reach only
anticompetitive schedule expansions. Such a rule, no matter how drafted,
would invariably affect at least some network programs valued more highly
by viewers than those that would displace them.

At best, a rule limiting the length of network schedules would have the
effect of halting exclusionary expansion while also inhibiting some schedule
growth that just as clearly serves the public interest. Of course, all rules
carry the risk that they will be counterproductive. In this case, three reasons
suggest that the risk is too high. First, our analysis of the economics of the
network-affiliate relationship demonstrates that no practical method now
exists whereby one can determine the "correct" length of network schedules. Rather, schedule length is a function of the competing relative values
of network and nonnetwork alternatives, values that will fluctuate con-

stantly as technology, viewers' desires, and advertisers' goals change. Second, even when network schedule expansion is profitable only because it is exclusionary, this tactic is not likely to be attractive to networks because those profits would have to be shared with, if not completely captured by, its own affiliates and other networks. The network likely will be at least as well off acquiring competing programs to maintain its hegemony. Finally, as new technologies grow and the relaxation of FCC entry barriers continues, the emergence of new outlets as bases for additional networks would overwhelm the ability of the three dominant networks to avoid competition by increasing the length of their schedules. For example, so many cable networks already exist that one is hard-pressed to imagine how ABC, CBS, or NBC could expand its present schedule to absorb a critical mass of each of these cable networks' programming.[20] Yet unless the bulk of competing networks' leading programs can thereby be captured, expansion will not produce foreclosure.

In short, that networks might expand their schedules to preclude or preempt competing networks is certainly possible in theory. A rule limiting the number of hours or programs a network can offer, however, is unlikely to deter such a practice and, at the same time, is likely to prevent programs that are valued highly by viewers from being shown. Such a rule could be rationalized, then, only by an animus toward networks per se, a position inconsistent with the public interest, or by the view that expansion profits networks at affiliates' expense, a view that is logically and factually erroneous.

Affiliate Compensation Plans

The suggestion that the FCC might further restrict graduated affiliate compensation plans—either by banning them altogether or by placing more specific limits on the permissible difference between average and marginal compensation—rests on a misperception. As we explained in detail in chapter 5, a graduated compensation plan produces the illusion that affiliates are first underpaid for valuable programs and then overpaid to induce them to clear programs inferior to nonnetwork programs. In reality, of course, the plan does no such thing because it cannot; except in extraordinary, short-lived situations, networks have neither the desire nor the ability to induce affiliate clearances that do not maximize the joint profits of networks and affiliates. What these plans do in fact accomplish is to separate the question of what network programs to clear from the question of how to divide the profits of that clearance between the two parties. The extent of graduation in the compensation scheme, then, affects only the relative profitability of the network and its affiliate, a matter unaffected by any public interest concerns.

Moreover, as explained above, many devices exist for evading the effects of a ban on graduated compensation plans. Networks can offer different rates for different dayparts, deductions from compensation for various incidental costs of networking, bonuses for affiliation renewals, and a host of other rewards that vary, explicitly or implicitly, with clearance levels. Because a rule banning or restricting graduated compensation would direct networks to act contrary to their perceived self-interest, they would have every incentive to evade the rule's effects by such devices. We can foresee no technique by which graduation can be effectively limited, short of governmental supervision of every burden imposed and benefit granted by the affiliation contract. No one has suggested that such supervision of approximately 600 affiliation contracts could conceivably be administered at any acceptable cost. Moreover, past experience with the enforcement of existing rules provides little support for the view that the FCC could detect and deter behavior designed to thwart its rules.

Finally, the emergence of additional commercial television networks counsels less, not more, regulatory intervention in this area. If the erosion of network entry barriers continues, this misguided notion that graduated compensation plans "coerce" clearances will surely dissipate as well.[21] If many rival networks exist, not even the least perceptive FCC Commissioner will be able to label a high compensation payment as an attempt to purchase exclusionary clearance rates.

Previewing of Network Programs

As described in chapter 4, proposals have been advanced to require networks to afford their affiliates opportunities to view network programs sufficiently in advance of their scheduled public broadcast so that the affiliates may arrange substitutions if they desire. Increased previewing might, it is argued, further the values of localism and competition.

The issue is a complicated one, requiring assessment of costs, benefits, and alternatives. Were networks to afford their affiliates no means whereby stations could learn in advance about program content, a case might well be made out for FCC intervention. But, of course, networks do not behave this way and, if they attempted to do so, affiliates would prevent it. Thus there is no need for a rule that simply requires that any one of several permissible types of previewing be offered. The question, then, is whether a unitary, rigid governmental rule is likely to strike a more appropriate balance between the burdens and benefits of various previewing options than would be achieved by bargaining between networks and affiliates. We see no reason to believe that any single regulation could be devised that could realistically promise such results.

Any proposal for a particular previewing rule must assess the costs and benefits of such a rule as well as the relative efficacy of alternatives. Previewing is not costless. If an affiliate's management is to preview a program, then someone must bear the costs of sending management to the place where the program is produced or stored or of sending the program, or a synopsis of it, to the affiliate. Further, those programs to be previewed must be guaranteed to be completed at some specified time prior to their general broadcast date; such a system will at least affect the producer's ability to make the program topic timely, as well as its production costs.

The benefits of a previewing rule would be the incremental change in existing behavior that the rule induces. When one considers the networks' incentives and practices, that change is likely to be slight. Networks, of course, have an incentive to obtain high clearance rates; but they also share their affiliates' desires not to offend substantial segments of the viewing audience. The dominant, conventional networks spend substantial sums of money closely supervising program production to ensure that it meets presently accepted standards of taste. In large measure, these expenditures are another economy of networking, with one entity performing a "quality review" for approximately 200 others.

To the extent that network previewing practices provide insufficient protection for certain affiliates, these firms have other options open to them. They may, as one group owner has done, send their own representatives to major production centers to observe program editing. They may take advantage of the previewing opportunities that networks already provide.[22] And, of course, the affiliate may rely upon the past performance of the program producer and the network. If either has misrepresented the nature of a previous episode, subsequent programs can be preempted or accepted only for delayed local broadcast after affiliate review.

Given these facts, the FCC would be hard-pressed to justify imposing a uniform previewing rule on networks. Affiliates are capable of protecting any interest the networks disregard and should be able to make their own assessment of the most cost-effective way of doing so.

Conclusions

Our analysis suggests that the network-affiliate relationship is overregulated. This conclusion is particularly compelling as we enter a period in which entry by, and competition among, television networks is increasing rapidly.

The root cause of these failures appears to be not so much misdirection of purpose as a failure of careful analysis. The Commission has been quite correct to focus its attention upon the question whether network-affiliate practices are exclusionary in the sense that they disadvantage potential new networks. Unfortunately, this focus has been so single-minded as to induce a form of regulatory paranoia. Practices designed to lower costs or to resolve debates over the distribution of profits between network and affiliate have too frequently been characterized as exclusionary or predatory. The true sources of network scarceness—FCC spectrum allocation policies, Commission hostility to pay television and nonbroadcast technologies, and the economies of full-time, nationwide, interconnected networking—have too often been overlooked. Further, the Commission has failed to recognize that its 1977 conclusions respecting radio networks largely apply to television today: most of the FCC's network-affiliate rules make sense, if at all, only for a system in which only two or three networks may operate simultaneously. As additional television networks develop, these rules become not only more obsolete, but more discriminatory and anticompetitive as well.

The lesson regulators should learn from reviewing these particular rules, then, is not that governmental network and affiliate rules can have no beneficial consequences, or even that the Commission has pursued unimportant goals. Rather, the FCC has failed to consider adequately whether its rules are likely to achieve those goals. Exclusionary practices can be avoided by sensible restrictions on multiple affiliations.[23] Monopoly practices can be effectively restrained by rules that prevent exploitation or aggrandizement of market power, such as the bans on affiliates' obtaining territorial exclusivity and networks' acquiring control over affiliates' advertising rates. When the Commission realizes that such controls would more effectively further the goals of competition, diversity, and localism, it should be able to perceive as well that its other rules have no more relevance to television today than they did to radio yesterday.

The largest barrier to achieving this enlightened state is likely to be the continuing, nagging fear that without the present rules networks somehow would dominate, exploit, or plunder affiliates. While the network and affiliate relationship has always been, in fact, cooperative and symbiotic as well as adversarial and marked by rivalry, that point is likely to be missed by those who confuse industry gossip about isolated cases with systematic analysis of aggregate industry performance, or those who do not distinguish between exclusionary behavior and bargaining over the distribution of profits. If, however, as occurred in radio, additional television networks are allowed to continue to enter the industry, so that a multiplicity of local outlets can turn to a multiplicity of possible network partners, that point should become increasingly evident even to the least discriminating observer.

7 Economic Analysis of the Relationship between Networks and Program Suppliers

The program supplier is the third entity, along with broadcast stations and advertisers, that the conventional television networks make use of to provide viewers with a national television service. Although the dominant networks produce some programs, especially their news and sports shows, they obtain the vast majority of their entertainment programs from independent firms. The principal business activity of some of these program suppliers consists of making television programs; many others are also major producers of theatrical motion pictures.[1]

Some of the fare exhibited on the dominant, conventional networks, and an even larger share of that shown by many cable networks, consists of "programs" originally produced for other "markets." For example, most theatrical motion pictures and many sports events are more or less fully developed presentations before networks acquire rights to broadcast them. Network acquisition of these rights, although not uncomplicated, has not been the central source of regulatory concern. Rather, regulation of the program supply function has evolved from analyses of the dominant networks' roles in purchasing programs specifically made for television.

Rarely, if ever, do the dominant networks purchase a program or series of episodes specifically made for television that was complete at the time of initial purchase. Rather, the networks contract for an option to exercise certain limited property rights, principally the right to first-run network television exhibition over programs (including series episodes) that are to be produced, usually according to an agreed-upon prototype or "pilot." These programs are not produced until this option is exercised. The networks finance much of the expense of program production, by agreeing in advance of production to pay a "license fee" for exhibition rights. Further, networks do not "own" such independently produced programs; they obtain only those rights surrendered by the supplier in return for the fee.[2]

In short, the network program supply process principally involves the contractual acquisition from independent entrepreneurs of certain property rights in creative or artistic works not yet produced. This acquisition process, upon which regulators have concentrated, simultaneously provides a method to finance or underwrite program development and production.

Structurally, the program supply industry is quite competitive. By any measure, concentration levels are relatively low and no significant barriers to entry exist,[3] with the possible exception of certain burdens (discussed below) imposed by the FCC's financial interest rule. Nonetheless, because entry into networking is limited and television programs are not homogeneous, the economics of the network program supply market are not simple. We seek to explain the manner in which that market works by first constructing a simplified example and subsequently adding more details to it.

Basic Determinants of Price
for Network Programs

We assume at the outset that there is only one network and that the only revenue generated by a program is derived from network sales to advertisers. Thus we ignore the existence of markets for the syndication of "off-network" reruns, for foreign distribution, for theatrical exhibition, and for sales to pay television distributors, although these assumptions are relaxed below. We also take as established the conclusion of all research known to us: that entry into the program production business is relatively easy so that new firms would quickly emerge if the profitabiliy of program production were to increase.

Given the assumptions of one network and many suppliers of heterogeneous programs, it is not possible to determine analytically the price that will be paid for each program. Because each program differs both in costs and ability to generate audiences, a program supplier may have some "bargaining power" in its negotiations with the network. In this environment it is possible to determine only the range within which the price ultimately can fall. Therefore, we discuss here the factors that determine the minimum price the supplier would be willing to accept and the maximum price the network would be willing to pay.

Supplier Reservation Price

Program suppliers utilize both labor and nonlabor inputs to produce programs. For our purposes, it is useful to divide labor inputs into two groups. The first, which for the sake of simplicity, we will call "production personnel," consists of stagehands, camera operators, film editors, and those engaged in similar crafts. This group constitutes a large pool of relatively homogeneous resources that are readily available to the industry. The second kind of labor input is "talent," which may include actors, directors, writers, and producers, and which is distinguished from production personnel in that these inputs are assumed to be heterogeneous both with respect to their "productivity," i.e., their ability to "produce" audiences, and with respect to what they could earn in their best alternative occupation, i.e., their opportunity costs.

For each program, which represents a unique combination of these inputs, it is possible to define the minimum price the program supplier will accept to produce and deliver the program. We refer to this price as the program supplier's "reservation price"; it measures the cost of producing a program when each input, including production personnel and talent, is being paid its opportunity cost. Resources that are new to the industry, for which there exist many close substitutes, will tend to have low opportunity costs since the next best employment opportunities for these resources may very well be outside the industry. On the other hand, some resources (actors, actresses, writers, producers, etc.) may have established reputations in television and related industries. These resources will generally command higher prices, reflecting their unique attributes and thus the higher-valued alternatives available to them.

Network Demand and the Determinants of Price

The maximum amount that the network is willing to pay for a program is determined by the revenue that accrues to the network as a result of purchasing and broadcasting the program.[4] This amount reflects the revenue generated by commercial messages broadcast during the program less the share of this revenue paid to affiliates who clear the program. It is also affected by increases (or decreases) in revenue generated during other time periods by exhibiting this program. The maximum payment a program supplier can obtain for its program is the differential between the revenue it generates as compared to the best alternative not acquired by the networks plus the opportunity cost of the resources employed in its production.

As an illustration, we list in column (1) of table 7.1 the gross revenues that each of four hypothetical programs would generate if exhibited on the network. Column (2) shows the reservation price of the supplier of each program, while column (3) shows the maximum potential contribution of each program to network revenue net of program acquisition costs. This contribution is the network's net revenue when program suppliers are paid only their reservation price [column (1) − column (2)]. Column (4), labeled "Differential net revenue," can be calculated only after we know how many programs the network will purchase. For example, suppose the network decides to purchase only two programs. After arraying all potential programs according to their estimated maximum net revenue, the network can find the two programs that are potentially most profitable (programs A and B in table 7.1) as well as the best program available to replace one of these programs if for some reason it is not purchased (program C in table 7.1). The difference between the maximum net revenue of a program and that of the best alternative program not purchased measures the differential net revenue for the former. For example, the differential net revenue for program A is 14 (70 − 56) and for program B it is 9 (65 − 56). The figures in column (5) represent the sum of the supplier's reservation price and its differential net revenue. Column (6) is the net revenue earned by the network if the supplier of each program receives the maximum possible payment.

Column (5), like column (4), is thus calculated using information for the programs that are potentially the most profitable for the network (A and B) and for the best available alternative program (C). If the network decided to purchase three programs instead of two, columns (4) to (6) would all change. Program D would become the best alternative program not purchased and the differential net revenue for programs A, B, and C would measure the amount by which the maximum net revenue for each exceeded that for D.

The figures presented in column (5) represent the prices of each program at which net profits on all programs are equated. Hence, they measure the maximum the network is willing to pay for each program. For example, if the network purchases only two programs, it will be willing to pay at most 44 for A since, if it does so, its profits would be 56 (column 6), which is equal to the profits that could be earned from the best alternative, C, when the producer of C is paid only its reservation price. Since program A has the potential of generating additional net revenue of 14 as compared with C, this is the maximum amount in addition to the firm's reservation price that the producer of A could extract from the network.

The precise price that will be negotiated between the network and the

Table 7.1 Illustration of the Determinants of Price for Network Programs

Programs	(1) Gross revenues generated	(2) Reservation price of supplier	(3) Maximum net revenue (1) – (2)	(4) Differential net revenue[a]	(5) Maximum payment for program[a] (2) + (4)	(6) Minimum net revenue[a] (1) – (5)
A	100	30	70	14	44	56
B	90	25	65	9	34	56
C	80	24	56	0	24	56
D	70	23	47			

a. Assumes network will purchase only two programs.

supplier will lie between the supplier's reservation price and the maximum price the network is willing to pay, and will depend on the relative bargaining power of the two parties. Relative bargaining power will reflect such factors as the number of buyers (networks) and program suppliers and the differential access of buyers and sellers to information regarding the differential net revenue that a particular program can generate. Where there is only one network (or where all networks act collusively) but many actual and potential program suppliers, and these suppliers are not able to estimate the revenues that their programs will generate for the network, the price paid by the network will approach the reservation price of each program supplier. On the other hand, if program suppliers are able to forecast the audiences (and hence advertising revenue potential) for their programs accurately, those suppliers offering programs whose potential net contribution to network profits is larger than other programs may be in a position to negotiate higher prices.

Two final points should be noted here. First, the decision concerning which programs to carry and that involving the payment to suppliers are separable. It is always in the network's interest to carry those programs that generate the maximum net revenue and there is always a distribution of these revenues between suppliers and the network which makes the parties better off than if these programs were not carried. Thus, there can be substantial variations in the share of profits that goes to suppliers without affecting the programs that are shown.

Second, even if suppliers were to receive all of the *differential* net revenues, the network would continue to retain some net revenue, as shown in column (6) of table 7.1. This residual is the result of barriers to entry into networking, caused by the limited number of stations available for affilation.[5]

The Effects of Increasing the Number of Networks

If more than one network exists, competition among them for programs will ensure that at least some of the differential net revenues accrue to suppliers even if they lack significant bargaining power or access to network net profit data. Since networks will be willing to pay more for a program so long as it yields as much net revenue as the best alternative program not purchased, bidding for the "best" programs will lead the networks to offer prices that approach the maximum they are willing to pay. If one network offers less than this, another can acquire the program by offering a higher price.

Another effect of increasing the number of networks bidding for programs, however, may be to reduce the amount of the differential net revenue and thus to reduce a program supplier's return. The size of that differential is likely to fall as the number of networks competing for viewers increases because the audience (and hence advertising revenues) each network can expect to attract is reduced by the entry of others.

Thus the net effect of the introduction of additional networks on network payments to program suppliers is the result of two countervailing forces. The proportion of program profits that accrue to the supplier will increase but the total amount to be distributed between the network and supplier will decline.

Summary

Economic analysis reveals that all television network programs will not necessarily receive an identical price because these programs are heterogeneous and network entry is restricted. Rather, the relative bargaining strengths of the parties will determine where, within specified limits, prices will be set. The lower limit is established by the supplier's reservation price; the networks cannot pay less than the opportunity cost of program production. The upper limit is the supplier's opportunity cost plus the difference between the revenue that program generates and the revenues the network would receive from the best alternative program not purchased.

Networks and producers will bargain over the distribution of this differential. An increase in the number of networks may, by increasing competition for programs, increase the proportion of the revenue differential accruing to the supplier but will also reduce the differential's amount.

The Effects on Program Prices of Acquisition of Other Rights

Syndication Rights[6]

Thus far we have ignored the possibility that exhibition rights to network programs can be sold directly to stations, in what the industry refers to as the "syndication market," after completion of the programs' network run. FCC rules forbid networks to acquire either financial interests in programs produced by others or domestic syndication rights in any programs. In order to determine the effect of these rules, therefore, one must examine the distribution of revenues from syndication under alternative settings.[7] First, we assume that networks are able to acquire these rights; second, we explore the effects of banning their acquisition.

The Effects of Permitting Networks to Acquire
Syndication Rights

The existence of a syndication market for "off-network" programs will increase the total revenues generated by those programs that have long network runs. We can demonstrate that the value of syndication rights is determined in the same manner as the value of rights to network exhibition, that is, by the differential between the syndication revenues generated by the program and those of the best program that is not syndicated. Column (1) of table 7.2 shows the total revenues, including syndication revenues, that would be generated by each hypothetical program assuming only one network and many program suppliers. Each entry is equal to the gross network revenue shown in table 7.1 plus syndication revenues of 10 for program A, 6 for program B, 5 for program C, and zero for program D. Column (2) of table 7.2 reproduces the reservation prices of table 7.1.

Column (3), labeled "maximum net revenue," is equal to the gross revenue, including that from syndication (column 1), minus the reservation price (column 2). It represents the net revenue that the network collects in the case where program suppliers receive only their reservation price and all other revenues, including syndication revenues, accrue to the network.

Column (4) shows the differential net network revenue on the assumption that the network is purchasing only two programs. This column differs from the corresponding column in table 7.1 by the difference between the syndication revenues earned by each of the programs shown and those that would accrue to the next best alternative program not exhibited, in this case program C. For example, the differential net revenue for program A rises from 14 in table 7.1 to 19 in table 7.2. This increase of 5 reflects the difference between the syndication revenues of 10 earned by program A and the syndication revenues of 5 that could be earned by program C.

The discussion of price determination in the absence of a syndication market revealed that program suppliers will receive no more than their reservation price plus their programs' differential net revenue. Since the addition of a syndication market does not affect the reservation price, program suppliers may share in the syndication revenues, but only to the

Table 7.2 Illustration of the Determinants of Price for Network Programs with Syndication Market

Programs	(1) Gross revenues generated (network and syndication)	(2) Reservation price of supplier	(3) Maximum net revenue (1) − (2)	(4) Differential net revenue[a]	(5) Maximum payment for program[a] (2) + (4)	(6) Minimum net revenue[a] (1) − (5)
A	110	30	80	19	49	61
B	96	25	71	10	35	61
C	85	24	61	0	24	61
D	70	23	47			

a. Assumes network will purchase only two programs.

extent of any differential in these revenues. Any remaining syndication revenues will accrue to the network. For example, even if the supplier of program A could capture all the differential net revenue, it would capture only half (5 of 10) of its syndication revenues. The network would capture the remainder. In general, the network will always be able to capture some of the syndication revenues, because without the purchase of the program by the network these programs would not (by assumption) be produced at all.

To summarize, a supplier will obtain from syndication no more than the difference between the syndication revenues its program can generate and those that can be generated by the network's best alternative. Adding networks and thereby increasing competition for programs has a similar effect on the size and distribution of revenues as in the case where the syndication market was ignored. Again, the existence of more networks may actually reduce the syndication revenues received by a supplier because an increase in the number of programs competing in the syndication market may reduce the differential net revenues for that program. However, the increase in the number of buyers increases the proportion of these revenues that the supplier can capture.

The Effects of Prohibiting Network Acquisition of Syndication Rights

The foregoing also reveals the effect of a rule that prohibits the acquisition of syndication rights by networks where, prior to the rule, the network owned all rights to syndication. For the sake of simplicity, assume the existence of only one network and the data in table 7.2. In that table syndication revenues are assumed to be equal to 10 for program A and 6 for program B, and under the rule this revenue must all go to the program suppliers. In the absence of the rule, the network would pay at most 49 (column (2) plus column (4)) for program A, including rights to all syndication revenue.

Under a rule whereby all syndication revenues go to the program suppliers and there is competition among suppliers, the supplier of program A will lower its price to the network by the expected present value of these revenues. In this case the price will be reduced by 10, since with one network the supplier received none of the syndication revenues. The supplier cannot charge a price higher than 39 because it would cause the network to negotiate with other program suppliers. The supplier of C could be willing to offer its program at 19 since this amount, combined with expected syndication revenues of 5, yields the supplier's reservation price of 24. At a price of 19, program C makes the same contribution to network profits as program A when it is priced at 39.

Thus we see that the effect of such a rule is to reduce the price paid for a program by the network by exactly the amount of syndication revenues the network would have received in the absence of the rule. The rule simply alters the form in which suppliers are paid, without affecting the total amount received. Moreover, the programs carried are also unaffected.

If the differential net revenue from network distribution is less than the revenues from syndication, the syndication rule would reduce the price paid by the network below the supplier's reservation price.[8] That is, the network will pay the program supplier less than its costs. But as long as syndication revenues plus the network payment equal or exceed the reservation price, the supplier will still be willing to produce the program.

Since there is no certainty that a syndication market will exist for the program, however, suppliers in such cases are essentially betting that future syndication revenues will be sufficiently large to offset the certain loss on the transaction with the networks. If networks were able to acquire syndication rights, program suppliers would be able to reduce these risks by selling their syndication rights to the networks in exchange for more certain revenues. As discussed below, an important effect of the ban on network acquisition of syndication rights, therefore, is to force the suppliers either to bear an increased share of the risk of failure or to find alternative ways of sharing or eliminating it.

Spin-off Protection and Options

Contracts for the acquisition of network series entertainment programs are usually written as option contracts. The option clause gives the acquiring network the exclusive right to purchase a series for a specific number of years—typically five in current contracts for prime-time series.[9] This option clause prevents the supplier from selling new episodes of the series to other networks during the term of the contract so long as the network continues to order new episodes periodically from the supplier. These clauses also purport to specify the prices that the network will pay for the series episodes in subsequent years, but this is not the most important aspect of the clause, since prices frequently are renegotiated.

Series contracts may also provide the network with "spin-off" protection, most often in one of two forms.[10] The supplier of a series may agree not to produce any derivative of that series without the network's consent. Alternatively, the supplier may promise only to negotiate first with that network should a derivative series be produced.

Shortly after the FCC prohibited networks from acquiring syndication rights in independently produced programs, the focal point of debate on the issue of network dominance over the program supply industry shifted to such contract provisions as options and spin-offs. Program suppliers claimed that networks obtained these rights at the expense of suppliers' profits, and the Justice Department asserted that obtaining them violated the Sherman Antitrust Act.[11] As far as we have been able to discover, however, neither the program suppliers nor the Antitrust Division offered any economic analysis of such provisions.

In fact, proper analysis of these provisions is formally similar to the preceding discussion of syndication rights and yields similar conclusions. It differs, however, in the factors that determine the value of these rights.

On the one hand, the value of syndication rights is realized solely from the additional audience exposures syndication permits. Since networks also obtain exclusivity protection for most entertainment series, which prevents episodes from the early years of a series' run from being syndicated while the network run continues, the network's revenue from its schedule is not affected by who owns the syndication rights. Consequently, syndication revenues are a net addition to the total revenue generated by a particular program.

On the other hand, the value of options and spin-off protection to the network results, in part, from the fact that without these provisions, a successful series or a spin-off could be sold to a competing network. Thus although ownership of these rights may increase network profits, as discussed below, a significant portion of their value may result from their barring the acquisition of very successful series or potentially successful spin-offs by competitors. Similarly, the principal value to the network of the exclusivity clause, as applied to episodes already broadcast, is protection against the possibility that the availability of reruns will diminish the audience for new (first-run) episodes.

We have already observed that a network will purchase a new program series if the difference between the revenue it generates and the supplier's reservation price is greater than that for alternative programs. Further, competition among suppliers and networks assures that the price paid by the network will be the supplier's reservation price plus the differential revenue generated as compared with the best alternative program not shown. To understand the bargaining process over option clauses, we must also recognize that if the program becomes successful, it will generate more revenue than originally anticipated. That program's differential revenue will be correspondingly greater and the network will be willing, if necessary to continue to exhibit the program in the second year, to pay a higher price equal to the first year's price plus the difference between the revenue anticipated at the time the first contract was negotiated and the higher revenues now expected in the second year.

If the network has acquired an option for the second year over a program whose performance has exceeded expectations, the program supplier is faced with the choice of selling the program to the same network, not producing at all, or obtaining a release from the option provision and offering the program to another network. Since the supplier cannot sell the program to another network without compensating the network holding the option, the latter is unlikely to pay its maximum price (the reservation price plus the new, unexpectedly high differential net revenue) for the rights to a second year and, in principle, it will pay much less. If the network and supplier finally settle on some price less than this maximum for the second year, then the network has gained as a result of the option clause. The value of the option will depend on the likelihood of its being exercised, that is, on the probability that a new program will be sufficiently successful to warrant renewing it for a second year, and on the savings to the network from having the option.

Having established the value of an option clause, the analysis proceeds as in the case of syndication rights. Competition among program suppliers assures that networks can acquire option clauses at a price no greater than the supplier's reservation price plus the differential net revenue produced by the program. That is, suppliers will not earn anything from granting options except to the extent that different programs have different revenue potential in subsequent years as perceived at the time when the contract is initially negotiated. If networks are prohibited from acquiring options, however, the purchase price for the first year will be reduced by *at least* the value of the option to the network, although, of course, it cannot fall below the supplier's reservation price. The reduction may exceed this value because banning the acquisition of options may discourage network participation in the development process (as discussed in greater detail below), and, if certain aspects of program development can be carried out more efficiently by the network, program costs may rise. Such an increase would reduce the amount to be divided between suppliers and networks and would likely reduce the amount obtained by each.

Spin-off protection can be analyzed in the same manner. The possession of rights to any spin-off puts the network in a stronger bargaining position when negotiating contract terms for a derivative program and thus permits the network to acquire it at a lower price than would otherwise be the case. Programs thought to have the potential for generating spin-offs, and for which the network acquires spin-off rights, will command higher prices in the initial negotiation with the network than those programs thought to lack such potential. Should spin-off protection be banned, the network would reduce the price paid for programs by at least the expected value of the spin-off protection. Once again, the presence or absence of a ban on spin-offs will probably not alter the identity of the programs produced for and exhibited by the network. A ban would only lower the prices suppliers receive from networks for programs with spin-off potential.

Exclusivity clauses also have a value to the network which can be estimated only at the time an initial program supply contract is concluded. Networks, therefore, cannot obtain these clauses "for free," but program selection will be affected by the program's expected differential net revenue, the cost of obtaining exclusivity.

The Effect of Uncertainty on Program Prices

Riskiness

To this point, the analysis has proceeded on the assumption that, at the time a network orders a program, it can predict accurately the audience that the program will attract. Clearly this assumption is unrealistic for two reasons. First, just as an oil wildcatter cannot be sure that all his drilling efforts will be successful and just as the head of a research laboratory cannot be certain that all his projects will produce useful discoveries, neither can a network program executive or television producer guarantee that every program will be a "hit." As in all nonroutine undertakings, some uncertainty is inherent in the process. Indeed, although considerable effort is devoted to the selection of programs, everyone knows that the process will produce some "bombs."[12]

The uncertainty described above is intrinsic to the activity being carried out, but there is a second kind of uncertainty surrounding the program supply process that has a different source. This uncertainty arises from the difficulty of ensuring that program producers and the resources they employ are producing programs most economically. Stated more concretely, a network may not be certain that all of the license fee paid to a producer will be invested in the production of the program or that the program will be produced at minimum cost. To the extent that inefficiency occurs, the quality of a program may be affected and, since it is difficult to determine in advance how much effort the producer will make to devote its revenues to most productive uses, this adds an additional element of uncertainty in predicting a program's audience.

These two sources of uncertainty broadly define the "risk" involved in the production of network programs. The implications of this risk for the relationship between network and program suppliers are considered here.

A Simple Analysis of Risk Sharing

We begin by limiting our discussion to the uncertainty inherent in attracting audiences. Consider a program that costs 50 to produce and is equally likely to generate revenues of 100 or 40. The *expected profit* of the program is thus

$$.5 \ (100) \ + \ .5 \ (40) \ - \ 50 \ = \ 20$$

Put another way, the program is "expected" to be profitable since the profit when it is successful (50) exceeds the loss when it fails (10) and it is equally likely that the program will succed or fail. However, the chances are even that the program will lose money. Consider three types of arrangements for sharing the risk:

1. The supplier is paid 60 for the program regardless of the revenue it generates.

2. The supplier is paid 10 less than the receipts from the program. Thus, if the program is a success, the supplier receives 90 but if the program fails, the supplier gets 30. In either case, the remainder, 10, is kept by the network.

3. The supplier receives 18 plus 60 percent of the revenues the program generates.

Each of these arrangements leaves both the supplier and the network with an expected profit of 10. The arrangements differ, however, with respect to the amount of risk borne by the respective parties. Under the first arrangement, the supplier bears none of the risk and is guaranteed a profit of 10. The network will either make 40 or lose 20, depending on whether the program generates revenues of 100 or 40. Under the second, the network is guaranteed a profit of 10 while the supplier either makes 40 or loses 20. Under the third, each of the parties bears some risk. The network will make 22 if the program is a success and will lose 2 if the program is a failure. The supplier earns 28 if the program is successful and loses 8 if it fails. Table 7.3 illustrates these alternatives.

If the network and supplier are concerned only with their expected returns, they will be indifferent to which arrangement is employed, although, of course, they will not be indifferent as to the precise amounts. In the third arrangement, for example, the network would prefer to pay less than 18 while the supplier will prefer to receive more—the form in which the expected profit is received is irrelevant.[13] Thus, if arrangement 3 is in effect and a rule is passed forbidding the networks from sharing in a program's revenues, arrangement 2 will be adopted and both parties will be just as well off as before. The only difference is that the network's profit of 10 is now certain while the risk to the supplier is increased. Where under arrangement 3 the supplier could either make 28 or lose 8, under the second it stands to earn more (40) if the program is successful and lose more (20) if it fails. The supplier's expected profit is still 10.

Risk Aversion

The situation is more complex, of course, if either party is averse to bearing risk, in the sense that it prefers a certain outcome to an uncertain one that offers the same expected return. Thus, in our previous example, if arrangement 3 is in effect by subsequently if forbidden by regulation, the parties will negotiate an arrangement like 2. If the network is averse to risk, it will be willing to accept a lower but certain return in place of the higher expected but uncertain return of arrangement 3. Suppose, for example, that the network will settle for a profit of 9 if its return is guaranteed. The supplier's expected return would rise to 11 in this case, but it is now more uncertain than it was under arrangement 3. The supplier now gains 41 if the program is a success, but loses 19 if it fails.[14]

It is thus important to distinguish between the distribution of the expected profit between network and supplier and the size of the "premium" charged for bearing risk. If both parties are indifferent to whether or not they bear risk (they are "risk neutral"), each would be indifferent to various alternative arrangements all of which generated the same expected profits for each party. If, instead, there is an aversion to risk on the part of one of the parties and the other party is indifferent to bearing risk, the latter will end up

Table 7.3 Alternative Distributions of Risk with Same Expected Profit

Arrangement	Network's expected profit	Supplier's expected profit
(1)	$10 = .5(100) + .5(40) - 60$	10
(2)	10	$10 = .5(90) + .5(30) - 50$
(3)	$10 = (.5)(.4)(100) + (.5)(.4)(40) - 18$	$10 = (.5)(.6)(100) + (.5)(.6)40 + 18 - 50$

bearing all of it. Since the risk-averse party is willing to pay to be free of risk while the party bearing the risk is willing to do so without receiving a higher expected return, both parties can be made better off when all of the risk is shifted to the risk-neutral party.

There is some reason to believe that the networks are more willing to bear the risk of program failure than suppliers. If a network purchases a large number of programs, it is able to limit its risk significantly in a way that a supplier of a single program cannot. By pooling risk, in the manner of an insurance company, a network may be willing and able to guarantee some return to suppliers even if there is considerable uncertainty concerning the success of any individual program.

Suppose that a network purchases five programs. If all the programs are like the one in the previous example, there is an expected profit of 100, or 20 per program. But although with a single program the odds are fifty-fifty that the program will produce a loss, the probability that all five programs combined will show a loss, which requires that all five fail, is only about three in one hundred, and this probability declines as more programs are pro-duced. Thus the network could guarantee a return to each supplier even though there is a fairly high probability that any given program will show a loss.[15]

When any return is guaranteed to a supplier, however, the second source of risk noted above (the problem of "shirking") may arise. The problem, well known to insurers as "moral hazard," occurs because insuring the supplier against the risk of failure reduces the supplier's incentive to expend resources in producing the program. As a result, the quality of the program may suffer. Thus, in our example, a supplier who is guaranteed 60 as payment for the program can increase its profits, at least temporarily, by spending less than 50 in production.[16] If the program fails, the network may find it difficult to ascribe the program's failure to the supplier's reduced efforts, because even the expenditure of the entire 50 would not have guaranteed the success of the program.

The effect of the network's guarantee on the supplier's behavior is dif-ficult to determine. It is somewhat attenuated by the fact that a supplier may increase the probability that the program will fail by shaving its costs. Moreover, to the extent that the network takes into account past perform-ance in purchasing programs, a supplier may choose not to jeopardize its prospects for future sales by such behavior.

Perhaps more importantly, the network need not and does not leave all production decisions to the supplier. Just as a fire insurer may inspect and require changes in a customer's premises, so, too, a network oversees and may require changes in the production of a program. In fact, throughout the program acquisition process, networks are closely involved in program development and exercise ultimate control over script and casting decisions.[17]

The above analysis points to two conclusions. First, because of the inability to predict precisely either revenues or costs, program suppliers will seek to have some of the risk borne by the networks and the networks will accept some of these risks because of their ability to spread the risk of failure over a large number of programs. Second, the networks will be reluctant to undertake all of the risk and thereby guarantee suppliers a return because of the fear that cost overruns will occur, or that the suppliers will fail to expend their "best efforts," or both. Consequently, suppliers are likely to share some of the risk that programs will fail and the networks are likely to monitor production closely.

The Effect of the Financial Interest and Syndication Rules on Risk Taking

The preceeding analysis of risk sharing enables us to explain more fully the effects of regulations prohibiting network acquisition of contractual rights from independent program producers. We elaborate these effects by analyzing a ban on the acquisition of financial interests or syndication rights because of the presence of such a Commission rule. The analysis applies equally, however, to any limitation on network acquisition of contractual rights (including exclusivity provisions, spin-off protection, and options) that shift more of the risk of program production to the networks in exchange for a certain network payment to the program supplier.

As noted in the preceding section, the division of risk between network and program supplier will be governed by three factors: (1) the attitude of the two parties toward risk taking; (2) the ability of the network to pool and hence reduce risk by acquiring many programs; and (3) the necessity of having the supplier bear some risk in order to prevent shirking. The division of risk agreed to will be reflected in the arrangement by which the network compensates the program supplier.

Prior to the financial interest and syndication rules, networks frequently paid a fixed license fee for the network run and shared the revenues of syndication with the supplier. The immediate effect of the rule was to reduce the fixed license fee for the network run and to channel all syndication revenues to the program supplier. Since syndication revenues are uncertain, another effect of the rule was to increase the share of risk borne by the program producer and to reduce the share borne by the network. However, in the process of shifting risk to the suppliers, the cost of risk bearing may have increased since the network's role in risk pooling is reduced.

To the extent that both the network and its suppliers are risk averse and must be compensated for taking risks, the increased payments to program suppliers required to compensate them for assuming more risk may exceed the amount the network would have required to bear the same risk. On average, suppliers will receive greater revenues than previously, with those suppliers who produce successful programs receiving much larger profits and those who offer unsuccessful programs suffering larger losses. But, if it is correct to assume that the networks are more efficient bearers of risk, the overall cost of program production will have been increased. Although individual program suppliers will now expect to earn greater profits (i.e., they will receive a risk premium for incurring this additional risk), this premium will be larger than that which would have been demanded by the networks because of their ability to pool risks over all programs purchased.[18] As a result, the network or the supplier or both will be worse off.[19] Moreover, there is no reason to expect that the allocation of resources will have been improved.

One additional implication of the above analysis is that there may be a tendency, as a result of the enactment of the financial interest and syndication rules, for concentration to increase in the program supply industry. Small suppliers who were previously able to shift risk to the network are unable to do so to the same extent. As a result, they may leave the industry, merge with other suppliers, or participate jointly in ventures with large suppliers in order to facilitate the pooling of risks. The size of the average supplier will thus increase and industry concentration will rise or specialized risk bearers will come into existence. It is interesting to note that since the rule's imposition there has apparently been a dramatic increase in the percentage of prime-time programs supplied by joint ventures between movie studios and independent producers.[20] Conversely, the percentage of prime-time programs produced solely by independents has undergone a marked decline.[21]

Conclusions

A number of significant conclusions emerge from analyzing the relationships between program prices and other contractual rights. First, prices for the sale of other rights such as options, exclusivity, or syndication participation are governed by the same principle that determines the prices for exhibition rights: the returns to program suppliers and the resources that they employ depend on the differential productivity of these resources, as well as the number of networks and the extent of competition among them. Further, the proportion of this differential productivity captured by suppliers is likely to be greater if that figure is known before the network agrees to acquire the series. Since it is common practice for the networks to acquire options to exhibit a series in subsequent years, suppliers and program inputs are likely to capture a smaller proportion of any unexpected renenues that the program generates.[22]

Second, if there is certainty about the audience a program will deliver, or if neither networks nor program suppliers are averse to bearing risk, the effect of a limitation on the rights that networks can acquire in programs is to alter the form of payment to suppliers but not the expected amount of the payment. Although suppliers must bear a larger share of the risk of program success, the limitation would not affect the programs produced and exhibited on the networks.

Third, if the ability of networks to bear risk exceeds that of program suppliers and if suppliers are averse to bearing risk, the effect of a ban on network acquisition of rights that have uncertain value is to raise the cost of program production. This results from the increase in the share of risk that program suppliers bear. Such an increase in cost may deter entry into program production by smaller firms or induce them to enter only by participating in joint ventures with larger firms.

Effects on Program Production of Network Acquisition of Exclusivity Protection, Spin-off Protection, and Options

The preceding discussion reveals that network acquisition of financial interests or ownership rights in the subsequent syndication of a program serves to shift some of the risk of program production from the program supplier to the network. In return, partial financing of the program is provided by the network to the supplier. In this sense, the network acts as an investing partner with the program supplier. Network acquisition of such interests makes the program procurement process more efficient because networks appear to be superior risk takers.

We also noted that acquisition of other common rights may serve the same risk-distribution purpose. In this respect, it is crucial to note that exclusivity clauses, spin-off protection, and option periods would remain an integral part of the contractual relationship between the network and program supplier even if the networks possessed no special advantage over program suppliers in obtaining financing for program production. These contractual provisions are obtained during the process of program development, as the "competitive" marketplace for new television program ideas is transformed into one in which the network and supplier are tied to each other by means of these contractual provisions. Option, exclusivity, and spin-off clauses result from the nature of the transaction between the network and program supplier in which the network buys not a finished program but a program idea. For these reasons, we believe these provisions are justified by reason of efficiency, beyond any function they perform in allocating risk.

The Role of Networks in Program Development

To understand this view, it is essential to recognize that a network performs more than a simple banking function. In addition to its role as financier, the network actively participates in the development of a program from its initial stages when a pilot script outline is drafted to the completion of filming the program series.[23] In this role of program developer, the network incurs costs involved in shaping the initial outline to meet the demands of advertisers.

Viewed in this manner, each network emerges as a partner with each of its program suppliers in the entire development process. The network and program supplier are coinvestors in a program idea, sharing the risk of loss and the profits of success.

In fact, the network may frequently be the most efficient program developer, a role that could not be assumed at lower cost by the program supplier whether financed directly by the network or by some other lending institution. One reason that the network possesses this advantage stems from the network's function as intermediary between its affiliated stations and advertisers. This enables the network to obtain information on the types of programs that advertisers and stations prefer and, more importantly, on the types of audiences that advertisers seek. Because they must collect this information constantly, the networks may be able to determine whether the idea offered by program suppliers will satisfy advertiser and station demands. The networks can then adapt the idea to the demands at a cost lower than that which program suppliers or other potential developers would incur in performing these essential tasks. Unless viewer program preferences and advertiser demands change only slowly over time, networks would appear to perform this function more efficiently than other potential developers.

The Nature of the Product Developed

The role of the network as developer of program series only partially explains the existence of those contractual provisions—such as options, exclusivity, and spin-offs—that constrain the supplier in the uses of its programs, particularly series episodes. One must also consider the nature of the product in question—the program idea—that the network wishes to acquire in order to understand such provisions fully.

Once the network has completed its investment in the development of the series idea, the revenues of the network will be affected if the supplier can then sell episodes to other purchasers. The supplier has an incentive to do so in order to increase its profits. Such behavior, however, may deter the network from making investments in program development. This phenomenon is a general, unavoidable characteristic of the marketplace for ideas.

Consider a firm that thinks an idea may be a commercial success and invests in developing that idea. If that firm does not possess exclusive rights to the developed idea, other firms may appropriate it. Since the appropriators incur no development costs, they can underprice the originator or match the originator's price and exceed its profits. A firm not granted property rights in the subsequent use of the idea will thus be deterred from investing in the development of new ideas because its anticipated gains from success are reduced and its risk of development increased. In the absence of some protection from competition, the incentive to produce and develop new ideas would be seriously impaired.[24]

One purpose of the typical network program supply contract is to protect against these risks. Although the property rights to a series concept initially reside with the program supplier, some of these rights are temporarily ceded to the networks during the program development process. At this juncture a series supplier becomes tied to one network for as long as that network continues to invest in the project and is restricted during that period in the disposition of that series in any manner not agreed to by the network. In return, the network advances the supplier funds with which to develop the idea and takes an active role in the development process.

The key point is that once this investment has been made, the series has value not only to the network performing this investment function but also to other stations, networks, and broadcast media. A sale by the program supplier to any of these other program outlets—after the network has made its investment—would reduce the network's revenues from the program and impair its ability to recoup its investment and development costs. Thus exclusivity, options, and spin-off provisions of the network-supplier contract may be, in part, necessary to protect the network's investment in program development and to provide a continuing incentive for it to do so. Moreover, given our reasons for believing that the networks are better suited for this investment-development function than are program suppliers, however financed, such provisions may be economically efficient.

Exclusivity

Without Networks

In order to understand the purposes served by exclusivity, we will focus initially on the rights to the first-run exhibition of a program where any cost advantages that networks might possess in program financing and development, scheduling, distribution, and the sale of national advertising are assumed away. Since individual program suppliers are as efficient as any other entity in performing these functions, there is no reason for the existence of networks. It is useful here to consider a supplier attempting to distribute a program that has already been produced (e.g., an off-network series or a theatrical movie). We adopt this focus simply to show that exclusivity could arise even in the absence of networks.

The supplier of a program can sell it to one or to several stations in each market. For a number of reasons, the supplier will often choose to sell the rights to a single station. With respect to the revenue incentives for multiple-station exhibition, it is instructive to examine first a polar case. Consider a group of programs, each of which is produced at the same cost and is a perfect substitute for all other programs in the group. By "perfect substitute" we mean that the total number of viewers watching these programs is independent of the specific programs that are exhibited and the total audience for these programs is divided equally among the stations that carry them. Because the programs are perfect substitutes, competition ensures that each supplier will earn no more than the cost of program production. Assume that there are no other program types.

If there are two stations in the market, the same program will be exhibited on both. The successful supplier will offer its program to both stations and charge each station a fraction of program production costs, with the total amount being paid just covering total costs. Competition among suppliers, combined with perfect substitutability among programs, ensures this result.

One way of characterizing this outcome is to note the condition required for multiple-station exhibition. If the additional revenues earned by a program from exhibition by a second station exceed the profits the second station could earn with the best alternative program, the program will be shown on more than one station. In our example, this condition clearly holds. The additional revenues accruing to a second exhibition of the program are one-half of total advertising revenues. The profit the second station could earn with the best alternative is one-half the advertising revenues less program production costs. The condition is thus easily met when programs are perfect substitutes. By exhibiting the same program on both stations, total advertising revenues are unchanged but additional production costs are avoided.

Consider a second example that is a bit closer to reality. Assume that there is a large number of programs each of which generates the same audience and that that audience is independent of what other programs are exhibited. In addition, there is another program that generates a larger audience which is also independent of the fare on other stations. The maximum price the supplier of the exceptional program can charge is the revenues it generates less the profits a station can earn if it exhibited an alternative.

Assume that the revenues generated by the exceptional program are $1,000 and the profits generated by each of the remaining programs amount to $100. If the supplier exhibits the program on one station, it will receive as much as $900 from the program's exhibition. The station will earn at least as much as it would have earned had it exhibited the alternative ($100). If the supplier instead considered exhibiting the program on two stations, each station would have to be charged a price that resulted in a profit of at least $100 from the program's exhibition. But, in such a case, the supplier would earn at most $800 ($1,000 − $200). As a consequence, the exceptional program will be exhibited on only one station.

The key to understanding this result is to return to the condition stated at the end of the first example: multiple-station exhibition of a program will occur only if the additional revenues accruing to the program as a result of its exhibition on a second station exceed the profitability of the second station's best alternative. In the second example, this is clearly not the case because (by assumption) the total revenue generated by the program ($1,000) is independent of the number of stations on which it is carried. Yet for each station that exhibits the program, the supplier must guarantee a profit of at least $100, the profitability of the best available alternative. Thus multiple-station exhibition, while not altering the exceptional program's total revenues, requires the supplier to pay additional exhibition costs.

We expect that multiple exhibition of a program will generally result in additional revenues. Some viewers who would have watched an alternative program will stay tuned for the exhibition of a program on another station. But, for two-station exhibition to occur, this increase in revenues must be sufficiently large to ensure that the second station earns profits at least as large as those from its best alternative. In effect, two exhibitions of the same program must generate greater profits than those from a single exhibition plus the profits from exhibiting an alternative. This appears to be a relatively stringent condition.

Thus, even where multiple-station exhibition increases revenues, the increase is unlikely to be sufficient to induce more than one station to air the program within a relatively short period of time. Moreover, there are additional costs associated with multiple-station exhibition that tend to reduce further the likelihood of multiple-station exhibition. First, additional distribution costs will be incurred in selling the rights to more than one station, since the program's episodes must be delivered to more than one station. Second, there may be promotional considerations that generate lower profits from multiple-station exhibition. The stations exhibiting the program in each market may be more efficient local promoters of that program than the producer (by virtue of the station's knowledge of local market characteristics). However, those promotional advantages may be eroded when the program is exhibited on more than one station, since each station would probably "free-ride" on the promotional efforts of others. As a consequence, the amount of promotional activity undertaken will be smaller than that which maximizes the profit from showing the program. One way for the supplier to eliminate the loss in profit associated with promotional free-riding is to sell the program to only one station in each market.

In principle, the supplier does have other alternatives that could reduce the extent of promotional inefficiencies associated with multiple-station exhibition. For example, the supplier could undertake these promotional efforts itself, but, as suggested above, the most efficient promoters may be the local stations. The supplier would have to expend additional funds in duplicating the knowledge of market characteristics already possessed by the local stations. Alternatively, the supplier could require each station to expend its "best efforts" in program promotion and then monitor each station's efforts to ensure that they are sufficient. This alternative obviously entails additional costs.

Finally, multiple-station exhibition may create uncertainty as to the share of total advertising revenues each station will receive from the carriage of a program. If stations are risk-averse, this uncertainty may tend to reduce the aggregate price that all stations in a market are willing to pay for nonexclusive program rights below the price that a single station would be willing to pay for exclusive exhibition rights. Exhibition of the program by a single station would eliminate this uncertainty.

While, in principle, the supplier could guarantee the share of revenues that each station in a market would receive (or, alternatively, tie the station payment to the actual revenues earned) if the program were exhibited on several stations, such an arrangement might be costly to negotiate. The calculation of the specified market share would have to take into account differences in the characteristics of stations, perhaps the most important being the so-called audience-flow effects. Some of the viewers of the program (if it is exhibited) may be tuning in because of programs aired earlier in the station's schedule. In determining the station's viewer share, therefore, the supplier would have to allow for the effect of this prior "flow." In a similar vein, the calculation would also have to take into account viewers of subsequent programs that are attributable to the supplier's program. At bottom, the supplier and the stations are interested in the additional revenues generated by the program for the station's entire schedule, as compared to the station's schedule with the next best alternative (substitute) program. Because these additional revenues will most likely differ across stations depending upon their particular schedules, the supplier will have to make the necessary station-by-station calculations. This solution to risk aversion on the part of stations increases the transactions costs of permitting multiple-station exhibition.

If the costs associated with the distribution, promotion, and risk of exhibition rise as the number of stations exhibiting the program increases, and if these higher costs are not offset by proportionately higher advertising revenues, then the supplier will choose to sell the exhibition rights to only one station because the supplier's profits will thus be maximized.

Note that for various reasons the grant of exclusive first-run exhibition rights is likely to be contained in explicit contractual provisions. In the absence of a contractual agreement that explicitly specifies the grant of exclusive exhibition rights to the station, the station must consider the possibility that, having purchased the putatively exclusive first-run rights, the supplier may then sell rights to other stations in the market. The supplier will have received all the revenues possible from an exclusive grant for first-run to the station and can capture additional revenues if other stations in the market are willing to pay anything for those rights. Other stations will not care what this particular station assumed in purchasing (implicit) exclusivity. That station will then find that it paid for less than it actually obtained and that the value of the rights it has purchased has dwindled. By "trusting" the supplier to behave as if explicit, exclusive first-run rights were sold to it, the station may find itself experiencing a loss.

As a consequence, all stations, in bidding for exclusive first-run exhibition rights, are likely to consider the prospect that the supplier will renege on an (implicit) exclusivity grant once the program is sold. Thus all stations bidding for the rights will be uncertain as to the precise revenues the "winner" will actually receive. This uncertainty will then lower the price stations are willing to pay for implicit exclusivity. Put another way, the greater the prospect that the supplier will "cheat" on implicit exclusivity, the more a grant of implicit exclusivity is similar to multiple-station exhibition. The supplier will thus receive smaller revenues than would be the case if the station trusted him. If, in addition, single-station exhibition maximizes supplier profits, the profits of the supplier will be reduced, blunting the supplier's incentive to invest in the same "quality" of programming in the future. The fundamental problem here is that it may be very difficult (costly) for the station to distinguish between "trustworthy" suppliers and others.

There are, of course, factors that will constrain this type of opportunistic supplier behavior, the most significant being maintenance of "goodwill" with stations in each market. But, given the flux in the identities of series suppliers, it is not clear how severe this constraint might be. The less severe it is, the more likely it is that stations will discount the prices they are willing to pay for exclusivity that is not guaranteed by the contract.

However, the supplier can assure the station that it will not engage in this kind of opportunistic behavior by simply granting the station contractually explicit exclusive first-run exhibition rights. Although such explicit grants are not without cost, they do protect the value of the exclusive rights purchased by the station from opportunism on the part of the supplier and thus preserve the station's incentives to promote the program efficiently.

The supplier also benefits from the contractually explicit grant because the price that stations are willing to pay will be increased by the inclusion of an exclusivity provision. This will act to preserve the development incentives of the supplier. Finally, the provision is quite easy to monitor.

Thus we would predict that, even in the absence of networks, exclusive rights of first-run exhibition would almost always be granted by suppliers or their agents (e.g., a distributor). Furthermore, we would predict that the exhibition of first-run syndicated programs, off-network programs, and theatrical films would occur under such contractually explicit exhibition grants. In fact, this is typically the case.

With Networks

Once we introduce the cost advantages associated with networking, the entire preceding analysis can be repeated by simply replacing "station" with "network." With networks, however, the efficiency-based argument for exclusivity becomes even more compelling. We argued earlier that the network and the program supplier are partners in the development of the program from an idea to a completed product. Given the lag between program development and exhibition, the network must purchase the program in the expectation that it will generate a specific but uncertain amount of advertising revenue. The absence of exclusive first-run exhibition rights, by reducing the expected revenues of the network from the program, would reduce the license fee paid by the network to the supplier. The supplier, as a result, would be forced to bear an increased share of the risk of program development and production. If both the network and supplier are risk-averse and if, as previously discussed, the risk-bearing function is more efficiently assumed by the network, the larger share of risk borne by the supplier will increase program costs. In addition, without an exclusive right of first-run exhibition, the supplier may enjoy the network's development efforts but sell the finished product to other purchasers. The reduction in the network's expected revenues caused by the prospect of such a "free ride" may reduce the network's incentive to participate in—and expend resources on—program development and may reduce the license fee even further. Although the supplier could undertake this function itself, we argued earlier that, by virtue of its knowledge of advertiser and station program demands, it is efficient for the network to participate in program development. If the supplier is compelled to assume a larger role, program costs will rise. For these reasons, the value of a program to a single network—and its supplier—with exclusive rights of first-run exhibition may be greater than the aggregate value of that program to all three networks and other purchasers without such exclusivity.

These reasons for the acquisition of exclusive right to first-run exhibition may explain other forms of exclusivity as well. Exclusivity with respect to the exhibition of episodes for which the network has already exhausted its exhibition rights and with respect to exhibition of new or repeat programs on other broadcast media enables the network to protect its investment in program development and to maximize the value of the program to both the supplier and the network.

It is also true that exclusivity provisions (and spin-off and option clauses) exclude purchasers willing to pay the additional expenses of distributing (or producing) a program's episodes, whether first-run or repeats.[25] But the additional expenses that other purchasers may be willing to pay do not include the development expenses previously incurred. If a network is unable to restrict the use of a program, the incentive for the network to undertake development is diminished because the expected revenues of the program to the network are reduced. In addition, program costs rise because the supplier must find additional sources for financing and developing a program, a function more efficiently borne by the network, and some programs might never be developed.

It is this development incentive that these contractual provisions protect at the cost of excluding purchasers willing to pay the marginal cost of distributing the program. But even in the absence of these provisions, the supplier will have the same incentive to maximize the profits of the program as the networks now do and to employ the same type of supply restrictions now embodied in the network-supplier contract. That is, even a supplier with total control of the use of a program is likely to restrict its use.

There may be instances, however, where the interests of the supplier of a particular series and the network diverge with respect to the timing of the release of a series into syndication. While the supplier is interested in maximizing the profitability of the single program, the network is interested in maximizing the profitability of its entire schedule. A supplier might argue that, long before its contract with the network expires, the release of previously produced episodes into syndication would not seriously divert audiences from new episodes of the program exhibited on that network. For example, because they are repeats, the episodes in the syndication market might attract smaller audiences and be exhibited at different times in different markets. But if the network permitted such an early release for all of its programs, enough of the network's audiences might be diverted from its entire program schedule to reduce significantly the profitability of program financing and development. Therefore, situations may arise in which it is in the interests of the network and suppliers collectively to release programs into syndication at a later date than the supplier of an individual series might choose.[26]

Spin-off Protection

A spin-off begins as an idea that stems from a series in which the network has already invested. Since the network may be partly responsible for the creation of a spin-off, the possibility that spin-offs may occur increases the incentive for the network to finance and participate in the initial development process. Moreover, as with the initial series, the network may be in the best position to judge the prospective success of the spin-off.

In one sense, spin-off protection can be viewed in the same fashion as exclusivity provisions. Because spin-offs are a derivative of the initial series in which the network has invested, the exhibition of spin-offs on another network may divert part of the audience from the inital series, reducing the value of that series to the network. This may be particularly true if the spin-off is based on characters from the original series. If the network is unable to protect its investment in the initial series, the network's incentive to invest in subsequent series may be lessened.

However, the extent of protection sought by the network with respect to the exhibition of spin-offs would probably be much less complete than that afforded the network with respect to the original series. The spin-off idea is largely a byproduct of the network's investment in the original series and the network does not necessarily undertake any additional investment in developing the spin-off idea into a series. Although spin-off protection in fact varies substantially across entertainment series, the typical right (particularly for prime-time series) provided the network is simply the limited right of first negotiation/first refusal.[27]

Options

Options allow the network, at specified times, to return the program rights to the supplier. Such a decision will be made by the network if further investments in the program are not expected to be profitable. If the network chooses to renew a series, i.e., continue its investment, that choice reflects the continued expected profitability of the program, which in turn depends in part on the network's earlier investments.

The network's role in program development is usually most pronounced, and its investment greatest, prior to the time the series is first exhibited and during the series' first broadcast year. It is during this period that network and supplier "flesh out" the characters, cast the program, develop the setting, outline the episode scripts, and, of course, make the pilot. Following the production of the pilot, network and supplier make further changes, and a process of fine-tuning continues throughout the entire first year of the series. The reason for this continuing investment is simply that the network—and the supplier—are interested in maximizing the profitability of the program, in enhancing its appeal to audiences and hence to advertisers.

These investment outlays are likely to be largest prior to and during the first season. Yet the revenues that accrue to the network will occur only over time. If the network were able initially to purchase only one or two years of exhibition rights, and had to compete with other networks for subsequent rights, the incentive of the network to invest in and develop new series would certainly be reduced. Although other entities would take over this function if options were banned, they may not be as efficient as the networks in doing so and might well demand options themselves.

If this investment-development role of the network is the underlying explanation for the option included in the network-supplier contract, one might predict that, for those programs in which the network's development role is limited, the option period might be absent or greatly reduced. Theatrical motion pictures are examples of such programs. Although the option period for entertainment series varies from four to seven years,[28] network exhibition rights to theatricals are usually purchased under contracts that carry no option clauses. This difference increases our confidence that the investment-development role of the network is the primary explanation for the option practice.

Summary

Each of these contractual practices—exclusivity, spin-off protection, and options—can be justified on grounds of efficiency. These types of practices are typical in markets of this kind. In any market of ideas, for the purchaser of the idea to have an incentive to develop that idea, his expected reward must be of sufficient magnitude to induce him to undertake the risks of development.

Of course, such clauses may have many effects, and networks may acquire these ancillary rights for a variety of motives. Some have alleged that

options, exclusivity, and spin-off protection, singly or in combination, reduce supplier's revenues or permit networks to monopolize the program
supply industry. These contentions can be assessed fully only after one
analyzes the Commission's 1970 program supply rules. The preceding economic analysis demonstrates, however, that whatever the purpose or effect
of these provisions, they are not "naked restraints of trade"; that is, they
serve, at least in part, the legitimate business purpose of stimulating an
efficient method of television program development. If such clauses were to
be banned or modified by law, it would be impossible to ignore the loss of
efficiency that would result.

8   Evaluation of Network–Program Supplier Regulations

Although the economics of the contractual relationship between networks and their suppliers are complicated, the structure of the program supply industry itself is easy to comprehend. Countless firms, of all shapes and sizes, supply or could supply network programs; entry is quite easy because no government license is required and the necessary capital investment is modest; and the nature of the production process is such that the product (taped or filmed programs) can easily be tailored by producers (or substituted for by purchasers) to reflect changes in the desires of the network, advertiser, or viewers.[1]

Networks deal with program suppliers as does any firm seeking to purchase entertainment programming. As we have seen, the contractual process is particularly complicated for those programs, produced solely for television, for which the networks also serve as financers and participate in the development process. The basic contractual arrangement, however, remains the fairly common phenomenon of negotiating a price in return for specific, limited rights to use and display intellectual property.

The foregoing suggests that any proponent of regulations aimed at the network-program supply relationship faces a considerable responsibility. As long as networks do not collude in determining what programs to purchase or on what terms, it is unclear how any particular regulation of these contract terms can further the goals of competition, diversity, and localism. With entry so easy into program supply and the number and nature of television networks dictated by other FCC policies, one can argue that these goals are achieved most directly by fostering unrestrained competition among networks for programs. Put another way, limiting the commercial terms networks exact from producers has no obvious effect on the extent of competition among networks or program suppliers or between the two groups, does not affect the number of outlets available to viewers or the extent to which viewers control program choices, and is unlikely to alter the networks' preferences among programs.

Nevertheless, at present federal regulation of network program supply contracts is quite extensive. Unfortunately, these regulations seem to rest not upon some carefully considered exceptions to the general principle that viewers benefit when networks compete for programs, but rather reflect ill-considered attempts to redress perceived imblances in bargaining power between the twin corporate giants of the American entertainment industry—the television networks and the major motion picture studios. Why the FCC and the Justice Department chose to expend resources mitigating the results of the competitive struggles among these firms is something we cannot explain with assurance. That these policies are misguided, and can easily be replaced by more promising and less cumbersome approaches, is perhaps best revealed by a closer examination of each of the principal regulatory policies now in effect.

The Financial Interest and Syndication Rules

Present Posture

The FCC has recently taken three actions suggesting that the agency itself is at present quite uncertain whether these rules serve any important purposes. In June, 1981, the Commission declared, in response to a CBS petition, that the financial interest rule's ban on network acquisition of "any financial or proprietary right or interest" in an independently produced TV program only prohibits acquiring the right to sell the program, through syndication, to conventional broadcast stations or to share in syndication profits.[2] Thus networks subject to the rules are not prohibited from obtaining rights to exhibit network programs on cable systems or to share in the profits from books, toys, or phonograph records that may be patterned after the programs. This construction of the financial interest rule makes it no more than an ancillary provision to the syndication rule. It apparently discards entirely the view that a more general prohibition is appropriate to prevent networks from using leverage, as purchasers of programs, to obtain concessions from program suppliers of rights in addition to those for network exhibition.

Four months later the Commission granted the Christian Broadcast Network (CBN) a waiver from the financial interest and syndication rules.[3] CBN was on the verge of becoming a "network" as defined by these rules, but convinced the FCC that applying them to CBN would, in fact, retard the network's development. In granting the waiver, the FCC made clear, once again, that the rules embodied no general principle as to how television networks should behave, but were instead designed to cover the conduct of only three corporations: ABC, CBS, and NBC. More importantly, the Commission acknowledged that, were the financial interest and syndication rules made generally applicable, these rules would probably thwart rather than promote competition by retarding the growth of new networks.

In June, 1982, the FCC issued a Notice of Proposed Rule Making that, if adopted, would repeal both the financial interest and syndication rules and the Commission subsequently indicated an intention to repeal the rules in the near future.[4] Twelve years after adopting these rules, the Commission finally asked the right questions about them. Do they "interfere with the ability of [networks and producers] to spread the financial risks and rewards [of program development and exhibition] in an appropriate manner"? Do they fail to "achieve any balancing of bargaining power between the parties"? Do they establish "an imbalance in the ability of networks and non-network outlets to compete for the products of independent producers"? To the extent that they attempt to protect suppliers "from undue influence," are the rules not "an appropriate subject of Commission concern"? As our analyses of the economics of the program supply process and the appropriate criteria for measuring FCC regulations demonstrate, each of these questions must be answered affirmatively. To see more specifically why they this is so requires a review of the reasons given for the adoption of these rules in the first place.

Initial Rationales

The Commission set forth three primary objectives when it adopted the rules: (1) to enhance the profitability of program producers; (2) to restrain or diminish the networks' bargaining power, resulting from their control of access to their affiliated stations, which was allegedly used to extract syndication rights and other financial interests from producers; and (3) to prevent the networks from favoring the programs in which they had acquired these interests.[5] All of these apparently distinct goals are, in reality, simply different formulations of the same general objective: to help program suppliers obtain larger fees for the programs they license to the networks.

We have suggested above that this objective serves no valid public interest because it does not advance the interests of viewers or foster competition among the networks. Moreover, as we will now discuss, the financial interest and syndication rules are unlikely to improve the profitability of producers or diminish the bargaining power of the networks. Further, although the rules, by definition, prevent the networks from favoring programs in which they have financial interests or syndication rights, the rules were unnecessary to accomplish this goal, whose attainment, in any case, would serve no demonstrable public purpose.

Producer Profitability

Neither the statutory nor the constitutional mandates that govern the Commission's responsibilities can or should be construed to authorize intrusion into the commercial relationship between program suppliers and networks for the purpose of enhancing the profits of suppliers. The FCC's attempts to justify concern with producer profitability ring hollow indeed.

The Commission sought to justify its efforts to increase the revenues obtained by network program producers on the ground that these additional profits would be used to develop programs for first-run syndication and therefore lead to more diverse program offerings and more competition in the production of television programs. This explanation may be sufficient to allay legalistic jurisdictional concerns,[6] but it makes no sense as a basis for adopting the financial interest and syndication rules. The program supply business is a competitive, adaptable industry that will provide programs of whatever type and quality the markets demand and will support. The number of first-run syndication suppliers and first-run syndicated programs increased after 1970 because the Prime Time Access Rule significantly increased the demand for such programs.[7] These increases did not occur because program suppliers obtained greater profits from the networks and used the revenue to subsidize the production of unprofitable first-run syndication programs. Simply stated, program suppliers are in business to make, not to dissipate, profits. If the demand for first-run syndicated programs is sufficient to make them profitable to produce, program suppliers will produce them. If such programs are not profitable, they will not be produced, regardless of the profits suppliers may earn from network programs, or from any of the other ventures in which they are engaged.

The Commission might be able to justify its concern about the profitability of program producers if the commercial practices of the networks threatened independent producers with extinction. Indeed, the Commission expressed concern in its 1970 opinion that network program producers were unable to recover their production costs from the network exhibition of their series.[8] This argument, however, fares no better when subjected to serious analysis than the one discussed above. The networks, obviously, do not want to maximize the profits of producers, but neither do the networks have any incentive to depress license fees to such a low level that producers are driven out of business. In the short run, such a policy would increase concentration among the remaining program suppliers and enhance their bargaining power in dealing with the networks. In the long run, the networks' primary source of programs would disappear completely.

Understanding this basic point about the relationship between networks and program suppliers helps put to rest the related issue of "deficit financing." Throughout the history of the Commission's consideration of the relationship between program suppliers and networks, few arguments have been as consistently and stridently urged upon the Commission as the contention that the inability of program producers to recover all the costs of program production from network license fees constitutes unassailable proof of the network's anticompetitive exercise of monopsony power. The fact that suppliers do not recover their production costs from the initial network exhibition of a program, however, does not establish that the networks either have or exercise such power. A television program consists of a bundle of property rights. The network does not obtain a license to all of these rights nor does it acquire permanent control over the rights it does contain. It would be surprising indeed if the networks, in acquiring the typical rights to two runs of series episodes, agreed to compensate producers for all of their production costs. One would no more expect the network to pay the full value of a series when such limited rights are acquired than one would expect the first person who leases a car to pay the entire cost of its production.

Thus the dispute about "deficit financing" is in reality another species of the more general debate between networks and program suppliers about the division of revenues between them. Program suppliers undoubtedly would like to obtain higher license fees for their programs, but they would not continue producing programs if they were not profitable.

In sum, the Commission lacks any basis for asserting that the financial interest and syndication rules are permissible because they increase the profits of network program producers. The rules cannot be justified on the grounds that they foster diversity and competition in first-run syndication because the profitability of network program production is irrelevant to a producer's decision to produce first-run syndicated programs. Further, the rules cannot be justified on the grounds that they will eliminate the "deficits" from network program production because those "deficits" result from the limited rights acquired by the networks.

Network Bargaining Power

Even if the Commission could establish some plausible policy justification for attempting to improve the profitability of network program producers, the financial interest and syndication rules will not accomplish that goal, as the experience of the past ten years has demonstrated. The reason is not obscure.

The program suppliers contend that the networks are able to obtain valuable property rights in programs for low license fees because they possess monopsony power.[9] But whatever bargaining power the networks possess derives principally from the fact that only a few firms exist that distribute programs nationally via interconnected stations. The financial interest and syndication rules do not affect this source of the networks' bargaining power, and therefore cannot be expected to reduce the extent of that power. Thus, even if one accepts the argument of the program suppliers, these two rules merely prevent the networks from exercising their monopsony power to obtain certain types of program rights. They do not prevent the networks from exercising that power by other means, and are therefore unlikely to alter the distribution of profits between producers and networks. As our economic analysis explains in some detail, the principal effect of the rules will be to reduce the license fees paid for network exhibition.

Preference for Programs in Which the Network Holds
Subsidary Interest

As a practical matter, the financial interest and syndication rules obviously do prevent the networks from favoring programs in which they hold such subsidiary interest. Commentators writing in the wake of the Commission's decision, however, have argued persuasively that the networks in fact never did favor programs in which they held additional financial interests.[10] Crandall has presented particularly persuasive evidence that the networks, far from favoring programs in which they obtained financial interests, actually may have been more likely to cancel those programs than ones in which they did not have such interests.[11] Thus, although the financial interest and syndication rules clearly accomplish the discrete, articulated goal of preventing "favoritism," it is unlikely that they have had any effect on the types or quality of programs offered by the networks.

In addition, it makes no sense to prevent networks from favoring programs produced pursuant to agreements containing certain clauses unless some public policy is violated by extracting the clause in the first place. Networks pay for financial interests just as they pay for promises to use a certain quality tape or film. No public interest is disserved by permitting networks to favor programs with a beneficial tape clause, and the same reasoning applies to programs whose agreements include financial interests.

Effects of the Rules

The conclusion that the financial interest and syndication rules neither affect the profitability of program producers, restrain the exercise of network bargaining power, nor influence network programming decisions does not mean that the rules have no effect on the relationship between the networks and program suppliers. Our economic analysis of the network/supplier relationship concludes that the licensing of various program property rights, including those within the scope of the two rules, provides a method for a producer and a network to share in the risk that a series will not succeed. The financial interest and syndication rules have had a direct impact on this risk-sharing arrangement.

If, as is likely, both the network and the program supplier are risk-averse, the rules oblige the supplier to assume more of the risk of failure than it ordinarily would.[12] As a result, the costs of program production will rise, since the producer must receive some compensation before assuming risk that would be more efficiently borne by the network. The producer will receive a higher license fee, but the additional payment will simply compensate the producer for the added risk. (This will be at least partially offset by any reduction in the license fee that results from the producer's retention of syndication rights.) Moreover, if, prior to adoption of the rules, the producer and network were sharing the profits from the program in some fashion, the increase in the cost of the program as a result of the shift in risk will reduce the amount to be divided between the parties, thereby rendering both the network and the supplier worse off. Of course, if prior to enactment of the rules the networks were able to reduce the license fee paid to producers to the minimum necessary to have the program produced, the added costs of the risk shifting would simply reduce the amount retained by the networks. The networks would be worse off, but the suppliers would be no better off.

The distortion of the risk-sharing arrangement is not the only inefficiency caused by the implementation of the financial interest and syndication rules. Prior to 1970, the networks may have acquired financial interests in certain programs in part because of the attitude of each party toward the risk of failure and in part because the networks are more efficient bearers of that risk. The networks are able to spread the risk of an unsuccessful series across the large number of programs that are developed each year. Most suppliers do not enjoy a similar advantage and the risk of failure each confronts is correspondingly higher than that faced by the network. By preventing networks from exploiting their advantage and bearing the risk of failure, program costs are likely to rise, reflecting the relative inefficiencies of suppliers as risk bearers, and neither the networks nor the suppliers will be better off. Indeed, the network may be worse off for the same reason suggested above, and the program supply industry as a whole may become more concentrated because large suppliers are better able than small ones to absorb the additional risk.[13]

Apart from these effects, the rules would have no discernible impact. As we have seen, financial interests and syndication rights are property rights that, prior to adoption of the rules, the networks frequently acquired. Like any other property rights, they were available for a fee and the networks obtained them by paying compensation to the program suppliers. By prohibiting the networks from acquiring these rights, the rules have the effect of reducing the license fee by the amount the networks would otherwise have paid to obtain them.

Thus the rules do not change the expected profitability of network program production; they only change the manner in which the profits are earned. By retaining all of the subsidiary program rights, the program supplier earns larger profits if a series is successful and incurs larger losses if it is unsuccessful than if some of these rights could be licensed to the network. The "expected" probability of the supplier, the amount of profit weighted by the probability of its receipt, should not change.

Summary

Measured against their asserted objectives, the financial interest and syndication rules have not increased producer profitability or diminished network bargaining power, nor could they. The Commission's opinion did not provide, nor have we been able to discover, a justifiable basis for the FCC's concern about producer profits. The suggestion that the two rules would foster the development of the first-run syndication market is a non sequitur. Moreover, the rules cannot be justified on the ground that program producers are incurring "deficits" to produce television programs, for that argument simply restates the truism that program suppliers would like to make more rather than less money.

Moreover, even if the Commission had a legitimate reason for attempting to improve the profitability of program suppliers, the financial interest and syndication rules are singularly ill suited to accomplish that goal. The networks can simply reduce license fees to reflect the fact that they no longer acquire the prohibited property rights. The rules are similarly ineffective in reducing network bargaining power, for the obvious reason that they do not affect the source of that power, the fact that only three networks exist. The networks are prevented from using that power to obtain certain rights, but are not prevented from using it to obtain other favorable terms.

Although the financial interest and syndication rules have not accomplished their objectives, they have had several undesirable effects on the network/program supplier relationship. The rules have disrupted a risk-sharing arrangement between networks and suppliers by prohibiting the use of the affected property rights to shift the risk of the program's failure from the supplier to the network. Because program suppliers have fewer series over which they can spread the risk of failure, they are probably less efficient bearers of the risk.

We should note also that, whatever effects the rules may have had, viewers have not derived any benefits from their adoption. The financial interest and syndication rules have not led to more diverse types of program on the networks or in syndication, nor have they increased the number of viewing options available to the public at any given time.[14] Indeed, the rules were not intended to achieve either of these goals. Given the present three-network system, the program offerings of the networks are intended to maximize advertising revenues. There is simply no reason to believe that even if the rules succeeded in shifting profits, program suppliers would not also continue to produce the same types of programs that maximize these revenues.

Since the Commission announced its intention to repeal what remains of the syndication rule, its proponents have advanced the novel contention that the rule is justified as a guard against monopoly, in that it prevents networks

from obtaining control over their closest competitor, off-network syndicated programs exhibited on independent stations. That argument is discussed, and rejected, in chapter 9, which deals with limitations on network
ownership interests.

We noted in chapter 4 that a recurring issue has been whether the financial
interest and syndication rules are broad enough. For all the reasons expressed above, we conclude that there is no reason for extending their reach.
If, for example, CBS wishes to acquire a program's cable exhibition rights at
the same time it acquires conventional network rights, the analysis is the
same as the case in which CBS bargains for conventional syndication rights.

For similar reasons, no one, to our knowledge, has seriously suggested
extending these rules to firms other than ABC, CBS, and NBC. Perhaps
nothing explains more forcefully why the rules are unsupportable. Ultimately, they do not rest on a belief that some public policy is violated when
an important network bids simultaneously for first- and second-run rights to
a program yet to be produced. If this were the rules' purpose, it should be
considered whether they should be applied at least to the large cable
networks as well. Rather, these rules rest upon the notion that public
regulation can usefully be employed to mediate disputes over the division of
profits between firms such as ABC and Gulf and Western, the parent of
Paramount Pictures. If the FCC does not redeem its promise to repeal these
rules, it will only be a matter of time until some reviewing court, noting that
the FCC has no justification for not intervening in identical disputes between Time, Inc. (parent of Home Box Office) and MCA (parent of Univer-
sal Studios), strikes them down as arbitrary and capricious.

Network Acquisition of Protective Rights

Analysis of the actions and further proposals to restrain networks' exclusivity protection, option clauses, and spin-off protection, described in chapter 4, does not yield conclusions as certain as those we advanced regarding
the financial interest and syndication rules. Acquisition of these rights
appears even more necessary to efficient networking than obtaining financial interests. But the possibility that networks may employ these rights to
exclude competitors is also greater. Accordingly, as in the case of station
affiliation agreements, a more delicate assessment of the relative risks and
benefits of regulatory oversight is necessary. When these are carefully
assessed, we believe a clear case can be made that neither the Justice

Department consent decrees nor proposals that the FCC adopt similar or more stringent rules are wise at the present time. We conclude, further, that the reasons given for these actions and proposals are unpersuasive.

The Functions of These Practices

In chapter 7 we provided a detailed analysis of the economic function of these protective rights, particularly as they appear in agreements to produce entertainment series programming. We observed that all three provisions serve, as do terms allocating financial interests, to distribute risks between networks and producers. But they perform additional functions as well. All provide efficient means to compensate a network for participating actively in program development and to protect its investment in a creative idea. Exclusivity protection further enables both network and supplier to maximize the joint profits from producing and exhibiting a program and to estimate the program's value to the network. Option clauses, when employed, also provide a supplier and its network with an effective means to structure sequentially the parties' respective roles in program development.

For these reasons, one must conclude that a principal reason for the use of such terms in network program supply contracts is to facilitate networking and to increase the joint rewards suppliers and networks derive from it. Indeed, even the most severe critics of these terms have never urged their abolition. Rather, opponents have argued that regulators should limit the amount of protection networks may purchase from suppliers by, for example, limiting the number of option years or the extent of exclusivity a network may obtain.

Arguments for Limiting These Practices

Redressing Imbalances in Bargaining Power
Opponents of protection assert that such limitations on these practices might be desirable for any of three reasons. First, the leading film studios have argued that regulation of option, exclusivity, and spin-off clauses will prevent the networks from realizing undue profits, at suppliers' expense, especially in the exhibition of those programs that turn out to be most profitable.[15] These clauses, the studios contend, enable the network to gain long-term control over programs at the early stages of development when their true value is not yet established. For example, a network may obtain,

at the pilot development stage, as many as six annual options at established prices plus exclusivity for a program that later becomes highly successful. The network payment specified in the original contract for the fifth option year may thus turn out to be far below that series' value in that year.

These contentions may be easily dismissed, for many of the same reasons we employed to dismiss similar arguments concerning the financial interest and syndication rules. No public policy is implicated by the manner of distribution, between network and program suppliers, of the profits from networking program series. Moreover, if suppliers get less than a "fair share" of these profits, it is because ABC, CBS, and NBC possess superior power because of their insulation from competition. Unless these clauses prevent new network entry (an issue discussed below), they do not grant or protect network market power. Therefore, if a regulation limits or abolishes these provisions, networks will employ their market power in other ways, such as by lowering license fees, to retain their "unfair" share of the profits. Finally, the contention conveniently ignores the fact that producers also enjoy market power by obtaining the exclusive copyright to their programs. Consequently, they can (and usually do) insist upon renegotiation of the license fees for series that are more successful than anticipated.[16]

Preventing Monopolization

A second contention, advanced by the Department of Justice in its antitrust suits against the dominant networks, is that these terms allow a network to monopolize the programming for that network. It is asserted, for example, that when ABC obtains long-term options and exclusivity and spin-off protection for a series produced for ABC, it thereby gains complete control over the market for (a) first-run exhibition of subsequent episodes of that series and (b) repeat or syndication exhibition of episodes already aired.[17]

That general contention has two possible specific meanings, neither of which is a sensible basis for regulation. One can view the Justice Department's contention as asserting that, by these clauses, only ABC exhibits ABC programs. Such an assertion is accurate, because it is tautological, but is quite irrelevant. Only General Motors make Cheverolet automobiles. To say that GM monopolizes the Chevy market is no more or less useful as a tool for analysis than to say ABC monopolized the business of the running the ABC network.

Alternatively, the Justice Department may have meant to assert that these clauses enable the network to monopolize the subsequent exhibition of programs that have already appeared on the network. The network monopolizes "used programs," as it were. That assertion mischaracterizes the program supply process or missapprehends the evils of monopoly. To say that ABC has a harmful monopoly on reruns of ABC programs must mean that ABC can prevent others from obtaining those rights. But any network is free to compete with ABC to obtain these program rights. That competition, however, will take place when the program is developed initially because, as we have seen, efficient network program supply processes often require that options, exclusivity clauses, and spin-off protection be granted at that time. If, like the Justice Department, we look at these protective rights only years after development expenses are incurred and the values of programs are ascertained, they appear to be inefficient, exclusionary devices. For example, one might notice that no other network can obtain rights to "Mork and Mindy" episodes if, three years earlier, "Mork and Mindy" was developed for ABC under an exclusive contract granting ABC six annual options. But these fourth-year rights were sold to ABC at a time when any other network was also free to bid for them. The allegation, then, that these terms are monopolistic is merely an assertion that the rights they convey should be sold at a different time. That assertion, in turn, is merely a rephrasing off the film studios' erroneous claim that networks acquire rights cheaply because they buy them early, not a claim of monopolization.

Preventing Exclusionary Behavior

A third reason that might be advanced for limiting options, exclusivity, and spin-off clauses is that networks may acquire these rights to forestall new network entry by restricting available programming. Certainly, as we have seen, these protective rights are granted by suppliers and obtained by networks principally to facilitate networking and to increase the profitability of programs for both the network and its supplier. But one might wish to distinguish between the time when these kinds of protective rights are exchanged and the precise extent of protection networks obtain from the exchange. A network might calculate, for example, that five annual options are necessary to justify its investment commitment, but decide to purchase two additional option years solely to assure that no new entrant could acquire that program for seven years.

Two facts counsel against acting upon this claim. First, none of these protective rights is a "naked restraint of trade," having as its sole or even predominant purpose suppression of competition. Rather, these contract terms, in some measure, appear to be indispensable to achieving efficient program supply. We know of no technique for measuring the extent to which the breadth or duration of a particular clause is necessary to achieve this end. Therefore, regulators could make only intutive guesses when trying to distinguish between "just enough" and "too much" protection.

Second, these terms are adopted by firms operating competitively. In ten years of effort, the Justice Department never obtained evidence sufficient to allege that the three major networks conspire among themselves on the duration or breadth of these protective rights. It is quite unlikely that the networks could, through merely parallel behavior, decide collectively how much exclusionary protection each would buy. Program suppliers compete, too, and the industry is unaffected by entry barriers. Thus any new network is likely to be able to induce entry by firms that will supply comparable programming. Indeed, a new network should be able to turn to the very firms that supply ABC, CBS, and NBC. These protective rights almost always cover programs, not suppliers, so that, for example, although CBS most likely obtained exclusive rights to "M*A*S*H," it certainly did not obtain exclusive rights to all programs produced by 20th Century-Fox. Many suppliers sell programs to more than one network.[18]

Under these conditions, the risk that regulation of options, exclusivity and spin-off clauses will do more harm than good is great. Further, the Commission has available alternatives that would strike directly, without risk of harm, at all the evils said to flow from these practices. The FCC can reduce the technological barriers to entry by new networks and then observe whether restrictive program supply clauses have exclusionary effects. Until this less drastic and more procompetitive alternative is explored, the case for regulating options, exclusivity, and spin-offs must rest, at best, upon sheer speculation.

Conclusions

The restrictions imposed by the antitrust consent decree on network acquisition of protective rights were defended by the Justice Department and the major film studios on somewhat different, but equally untenable, theories. These terms do not permit networks to exact unconscionably low prices from program suppliers or to monopolize entertainment series programs.

Had these devices been analyzed more carefully, however, a more plausible cause for concern might have emerged. These devices might represent, at the extreme, exclusionary behavior designed to handicap potential new networks by tying up programming for an unduly long period. No systematic or sensible assessment of that issue is possible, however, until the FCC first takes the less drastic and undeniably procompetitive step of removing technological and regulatory barriers to new networks. Experience under that system should demonstrate whether competition will erode any possibility of these clauses being unduly restrictive or whether a limited regulatory oversight is necessary.

The Prime Time Access Rule

The Prime Time Access Rule (PTAR) best illustrates our assertion that a key to measuring the utility of network regulation is establishing what regulatory goals are permissible. PTAR is a fairly straightforward rule, easily comprehensible and producing fairly predictable results (although the FCC that promulgated PTAR seriously misjudged its probable effects). But normative evaluations or PTAR's performance frequently resemble explications of the physical properties of a Rube Goldberg invention, because these evaluations treat every effect of the rule as a reason for retaining it. If an infinite variety of regulatory ends are desirable, then PTAR is an unqualified success. By the standards we delineated and defended in chapter 3, the rule has nothing to commend it.

PTAR's Effects

The Prime Time Access Rule provides that network affiliates located in the fifty largest markets may carry no more than three hours of network entertainment programming, or off-network syndicated programs, during the four prime-time hours each night. Several consequences ensued from PTAR's promulgation.

ABC, CBS, and NBC ceased to program one hour per night, six days a week, because none found it profitable to operate a network reaching only the one-third of U.S. viewers residing outside the top fifty markets.[19] All three chose to vacate the same time period because, in a subsequent semiformal letter, the FCC told them to.[20] The networks may actually have profited from this govenment-orchestrated joint schedule reduction because it decreased the inventory of prime-time commercial minutes each had available for sale.

Producers of first-run syndicated programming received a virtually cap-tive market. During that period, only they could offer affiliates programs that spread programming costs over many stations. No mechanism arose for harnessing the ability of geographically dispersed network affiliates to finance, develop, and distribute new, widely cleared, first-run programs for the access period, as ABC, CBS, and NBC do for other time periods. The FCC's spectrum allocation plan assured that no firm could grow from an access-period network to a fourth full-scale, full-time network; moreover, there is little efficiency in utilizing all affiliates' resources to develop only six hours of network programs per week.[21] Therefore, these new syndicated programs reached fewer stations than did network programs. Conse-quently, each program earned less money and had to be more cheaply produced. For all these reasons, the access period, quite predictably, be-came dominated by variations of network daytime programs ("Tic Tac Dough," "The Newlywed Game") because these were cheap by prime-time standards and had been created initially with network financial and develop-mental resources, by new versions of cheaper former network prime-time series that had been dropped when network schedules were reduced by PTAR ("Lawrence Welk," "Hee Haw"), and by inexpensive talk shows ("P.M. Magazine," "Entertainment Tonight").

Independent stations made more money after PTAR because they could show popular off-network syndicated series without competition from first-run network programs. Network affiliates, to their surprise, realized higher profits, too. PTAR dictated what those affiliates previously could not achieve without illegal overt collusion: mutual, roughly equal, reductions in expenditures on program quality by the three dominant firms in each view-ing locality. Happily for them, viewership did not decline as fast as those expenses.

Policy Implications

The foregoing effects are all fairly predictable consequences of declaring one prime-time hour off-limits to the dominant networks and are therefore likely to continue. These effects also explain both why the television indus-try for the most part has embraced the rule (although the networks now oppose it) and why PTAR nevertheless serves no defensible public purpose. Many industry members like PTAR because they are wealthier with it than without it. The rule should be discarded because it serves no interests of the viewing public.

Initial Justification

When the FCC promulgated the rule, it expressed the hope that PTAR would stimulate production of network quality syndicated prime-time programs, thereby enhancing competition among program suppliers and between networks and program suppliers.

Unfortunately, this hope rested upon a fundamental misapprehension of the economics of networking. Apparently confusing correlation with cause and effect, the Commission believed that network quality programs are a function of the time period in which they are shown. But ABC, CBS, and NBC do not succeed because they distribute expensive first-run situation comedy and dramatic series. Rather, their success in taking advantage of the efficiences resulting from a national, interconnected, full-time system of program distribution has enabled the networks to compete among themselves by offering such programs. A firm not enjoying these economies cannot profitably produce and distribute these programs.

The Case against PTAR

Apparently recognizing that early hopes for the rule rested on false premises, the Commission and other PTAR supporters have cast about for additional justifications. In this process, the case for the rule has assumed such complexity that no one could answer directly every assertion of PTAR's defenders. The principal point, rather, is that no specific, permissible regulatory purpose is furthered by the rule.

PTAR does not promote competition. Indeed, as noted, it suppresses competition among networks, among stations, and among program suppliers. PTAR does not promote diversity, as we have defined it. Viewers have no more viewing options at 7:30 P.M. than they do at 9:30 P.M. If program type or content is the measure of diversity, then PTAR achieves that goal only insofar as it necessitates that stations broadcast less expensive programs than those viewers would otherwise choose to watch. PTAR fosters community localism only in any fortuitous instances in which affiliates find locally produced programs more profitable than first-run syndicated programs but less remunerative than network programs, whether first-run or rerun. Individual localism is directly thwarted by PTAR. Viewers are prevented from choosing first-run network programs or (on 150 affiliates) off-network syndicated fare.

Typical Defenses Offered Today

That the public interest could be served by preventing the viewing public from choosing what it wishes to see is, at best, an odd proposition. Defenders of PTAR, therefore, are likely to express their arguments another way.

Restructured syndication market. Some argue that the syndication market has been improved. The only change PTAR induced, however, was in the amount of profits that market generates. The syndication market was competitively structured and devoid of entry barriers before the Commission adopted the rule.[22]

Reduction in network dominance. Others note that "network dominance" has been reduced. But that is true only in the sense that ABC, CBS, and NBC now develop and distribute fewer programs. We have already explained why an opposition to networking per se lacks any public policy justification.

Enhanced affiliate discretion. Yet other PTAR defenders observe that affiliated stations have been encouraged to exercise their own discretion in selecting the programs they exhibit. But, as we have seen, these affiliates exercise choice during nonaccess time as well. In truth, the claim that discretion has been enhanced amounts to saying that affiliates have been enabled to choose cheap programming without fear that a competitor will offer viewers more attractive fare. Public policy should oppose, not protect, such discretion.

Summary

The foregoing arguments for PTAR are all to the same effect: PTAR fulfills its purposes because the purpose of PTAR is to exist. The fundamental problem remains, however, that neither the increased exhibition of first-run syndicated programs and consequent diminution of network programs nor the restriction on affiliates' discretion can be linked to any sensible or permissible regulatory goal. Moreover, if these consequences of PTAR are, in truth, public benefits, then the case for extending the rule—throughout prime-time and into daytime and, perhaps, late-night programming—would be irresistible. In fact, however, no public official has ever made such a suggestion because none can imagine that a rule designed to cut network schedules, simply for the sake of cutting network schedules and thereby redistributing industry income, could be justified by any public policy expressed in the Communications Act.

For the same reasons, no one has urged that the rule be applied to new networks. Indeed, when the Christian Broadcasting Network was on the verge of attaining such size that is would be covered by PTAR, the FCC promptly waived CBN's obligation to comply with the rule.[23] Few actions would be more likely to stunt the growth of developing networks than depriving them of the opportunity to compete for viewers during all of prime-time.

As these new networks grow, even affiliates of ABC, CBS, and NBC will clamor for PTAR's repeal as they suffer viewer defections during the access period. At that time, the Commission will have no choice but to repeal the rule, for its political support will have vanished along with its asserted rationale.

Conclusions

Unlike regulations of the network-affiliate relationship, federal rules aimed at the program supply process have been fundamentally misguided. Regulators have sought two ends: the unattainable and impermissible goal of altering the division of revenues between networks and program suppliers by dictating one or two terms in complex contracts, and the elitist and impermissible goal of denying viewers the option to watch network programming.

We do not pretend to be able to discover the motivations that produced these regulatory initiatives. Analytically, they appear to stem from a failure to appreciate the economics of networking and the source of entry barriers to new networks. Had the FCC and the Department of Justice understood these economic facts of life, they could have developed a set of principles, much easier to enforce than present regulations, that would also have protected fully the public interest in network acquisition of programs from a competitive program supply industry.

Two principles should govern. First, networks must not collude in selecting programs or establishing the terms on which they will bid for them. Second, networks with substantial market power should not be permitted to obtain long-term exclusivity provisions whose only purpose is exclusionary or whose effects are likely to be so, where these conclusions are apparent in light of the duration of the provision and an inability of other firms to offer similar (but not identical) programs. None of the entertainment program acquisition practices of ABC, CBS, and NBC examined to date appears to violate these principles. Only the most careful observation, however, can be effective against collusion. And the second principle is much more likely to be threatened by practices in unexamined program areas where artificial entry barriers are maintained by law, such as sports events.

Within the bounds established by these principles, the public interest in competition, diversity, and localism will best be served by permitting networks to compete in acquiring programs, while reducing the barriers to new network entry. In a sense, regulators already understand this point intuitively, for none has proposed applying existing restrictions to any network other than ABC, CBS, and NBC. When regulators (or federal judges reviewing them) finally grasp the reasons why PTAR should not cover the Cable News Network, and why Home Box Office should not be saddled with the syndication rule, then they will realize as well that the rules are no more justifiable as applied to ABC, CBS, and NBC.

The point is not that ABC, CBS, and NBC have produced such exciting, outstanding, or culturally uplifting programs that we should ask for more. Far from it. Rather, the truth is that the economic advantages network distribution possesses over syndication have determined the current structure of U.S. commercial television program offerings. To attempt to alter the outcomes of the present system without addressing the more basic causes of dominance by three networks is a Sisyphean task. If these causes are addressed, however, viewers may be able to realize both the economic and the cultural promise television offers.

9   Ownership Restrictions

Our analysis to this point has described the principles that should govern regulation of television networks' commercial dealings with independent firms. However, networks themselves may also perform the same functions that independent firms often carry out. For example, networks can produce programs rather than acquire them from motion picture studios or other producers. Or networks may own the outlets through which their programs are broadcast locally. Moreover, if permitted, a single firm may choose to operate more than a single network.

The purpose of this chapter is to develop principles that should govern regulation of commercial television network ownership practices. It seeks to determine what limits, if any, should be placed on the size or structure of firms engaged in networking television programs. Although this question is different in form from the issues examined previously, much of the earlier analysis of contract regulation applies to ownership restrictions as well.

Potential Types of Ownership Restrictions

The problem of devising a sensible policy toward network structure can be reduced to manageable proportions by considering the functions networks perform within the television industry. Networks essentially act as middlemen, acquiring programs from independent suppliers, arranging for interconnection, delivering schedules to local broadcast outlets, and selling time to advertisers. It follows that a network, in its capacity as such, can expand its market power or exclude potential new network entrants only by gaining control over other networks or over firms providing one of the functions that networks mediate.

Of course, no firm can "acquire" viewers, who remain free to turn the TV dial, whether they do so or not. Nor could a network acquire sufficient commercial advertisers to eliminate other networks from the advertising market. Theoretically, in the past a network might have been able to conrol the interconnection function by acquiring AT&T, but FCC regulations historically have required such services to be provided on a common-carrier basis.[1] More recently, as many firms have entered the long-distance trans-mission business, monopolization of networking through control of some interconnection facilities seems an especially unlikely possibility.

The real issues, then, are what limits, if any, should be placed on televi-sion networks' freedom to acquire or control (1) local broadcast outlets, (2) television programs or their suppliers or (3) other networks. If these issues are resolved in a manner that prevents network monopolization of these functions, then the number and size of television networks will depend solely on the levels of viewer and advertiser demand for network programs, the number of outlets and programs available, and the relative attractive-ness of the networks' schedules and the efficiency with which they are assembled. Such a result would satisfy, as far as is possible, the criteria developed in chapter 3 for measuring whether television network structure and behavior serve the public interest.

Existing Ownership Restrictions

Federal regulations of network structure presently stem from one of two sources: FCC rules and the provisions of the antitrust consent decrees obtained by the Department of Justice from ABC, CBS, and NBC. Collec-tively, they impose the following restrictions on network expansion into the three functions just identified.

Local Outlets

No rule specifically applicable only to networks governs ownership of conventional broadcast staions. Two FCC rules, however, apply to all station owners, including networks. First, nationwide, no firm may own or control more than five VHF stations or more than seven VHF and UHF stations, although the Commission is considering whether to repeal this rule.[2] At present, ABC, CBS, and NBC each own five VHF stations and no UHF licensees. Second within each local market, no firm may own or control more than one television station, the so-called duopoly rule.[3] Addi-tionally, the FCC has prohibited ABC, CBS, and NBC—but no other firm, network or otherwise (except colocated broadcast stations and telephone companies)—from owning any cable system.[4] The Commission has, however, recently proposed to repeal this "network-cable cross-ownership" rule.[5]

Programs

The FCC has never limited the number of program suppliers or network programs that a network may own or control. As we have observed, however, the Commission's syndication rule has the effect of prohibiting ownership of, or control over, off-network program rights by ABC, CBS, and NBC. The Commission could have interpreted the financial interest rule to limit substantially the range of interests these networks could acquire in independently produced programs. Instead, the FCC construed that rule to forbid only the acquisition of profit shares in syndication revenues.[6]

The antitrust consent decrees extensively limit the amount of entertainment programming that ABC, CBS, or NBC may produce themselves.[7] For example, none of these firms may produce more than 2.5 hours per week of prime-time entertainment programming. The restrictions, all of which remain in effect for ten years from the date of the decrees, impose different limits for programs produced for other dayparts.

Networks

The FCC forbids anyone to operate simultaneously, and in the same local geographic market, more than one television network.[8] For purposes of this rule, a "network" is any firm offering programs to two or more interconnected broadcast stations. The Commission initially adopted this "dual networking" prohibition to force NBC to divest one of its co-owned Red and Blue radio networks, but the rule was abandoned with respect to radio in 1977.[9]

Network Ownership of Local Outlets

Broadcast Stations

When a conventional network seeks to acquire a conventional broadcast station, the relevant policy conclusions may be easily stated because they have already been indentified. The conclusions are those that emerge from the examination of the network-affiliate relationship in chapters 5 and 6.

In principle, as we observed in those chapters, networks can control outlets by contract as well as by ownership. Our empirical study of clearance patterns revealed that, in practice, ownership produces slightly higher rates of network program clearance. These differences probably are largely the result of FCC regulations and strategic bargaining over profit distribution that can affect behavior only when network and station are linked by contract. Neither those regulations nor such strategic bargaining advances the public interest according to the criteria specified in chapter 3, so no public value is disserved by the slight increase in network program clearances that has accompanied network ownership of stations. Conceivably, the public is better served as a result.

As the economic analysis of the network-affiliate relationship explains, a network acting as a station owner has no incentive to clear unprofitable network programs. Nor, in the absence of FCC constraints and the vagaries of strategic bargaining, is the network less able to induce station clearances when it is merely a contractual partner, rather than an owner, of an affiliated station. Consequently, no issues of diversity or localism are implicated by the difference between network ownership or contractual affiliation.

The question remains whether network ownership of stations might be anticompetitive, enabling the network to block, or raise the cost of, entry by additional networks. That question is no different from the issue, analyzed in detail in chapter 6, of whether networks' contractual restraints on affiliates could have these exclusionary effects. The same answers apply. First, ownership, like exclusive affiliation or option time, is unlikely to be an effective or efficient exclusionary device. Second, such a tactic could be successful only if a network ties up multiple outlets in key strategic markets. This tactic is prevented by the FCC's duopoly rule but would also be prevented by a less draconian rule, which we recommend below, forbidding any firm from acquiring avoidable power in local markets.

For these reasons, the public interest would not be furthered by flatly prohibiting networks from owning conventional broadcast stations. Prudence does justify, however, continuing a policy that prevents networks from owning or affiliating with more than one station in a market where those stations might jointly exercise market power.[10]

Cable Systems

The FCC's rule forbidding the three dominant networks from acquiring cable systems is more difficult to evaluate. Because those networks' programs are broadcast over conventional stations, the source of the Commission's opposition to network ownership of cable systems is not intuitively obvious. Indeed, the FCC promulgated the rule in 1970 without disclosing previously that such a rule was under consideration and without any explanation at the time of its basis or purpose.[11] Certainly the Commission has never undertaken to provide any empirical measurement of the rule's effects or any economic explanation of its intended results.

In these circumstances, the best one can do is to scrutinize the Commission's latest pronouncement on the matter, the notice of its proposal to repeal the rule.[12] There the agency asserted that the rule might serve any of three purposes. None withstands critical analysis.

First, the rule might prevent national concentration in cable system ownership. Indeed, it is possible that the rule forestalled ABC, CBS, and NBC from acquiring many cable systems during the 1970s, although we are aware of no evidence that any of these firms ever planned such extensive acquisitions. Today, however, cable system ownership is, by any measure, quite unconcentrated.[13] In any event, excluding potential additional cable system owners is hardly likely to reduce concentration in the future.

Alternatively, the rule might be designed to prevent ABC, CBS, and NBC from gaining an undue share of the overall video market, a market that includes at least both cable and conventional broadcast outlets. Certainly the public interest in futhering competition is served by avoiding such a result. Moreover, network ownership of a cable system might reduce competition. Consider, for example, a local video market containing only three television stations and one cable system. Were NBC to acquire or affiliate with one of the stations and purchase the cable system, the resulting concentration might give NBC substantial local market power.

This rationale, however, is entirely speculative and, even if accepted, the rule is both overbroad and underinclusive for these purposes. No one, least of all the FCC, has ever clearly defined a local video market or indicated how to measure concentration within it. Is the local video market the sum of activated channels that viewers in fact receive? Or does it include those channels that could be received if viewers subscribed to them? In either event, does it include viewer-activated channels (such as those provided by renting or purchasing videocassettes) or potentially available channels (such as those served by direct broadcat satellites)? Are market shares to be measured in dollars rather than viewers or channels? If so, does the market consist of total receipts, including advertiser, viewer and public expenditures? Again, does it include actual revenues from videocassettes and potential income from emerging technologies?

We do not pretend to be able to answer these questions at this time, but the important point is that the FCC has not answered them either. In the absence of such answers, however, no rational claim can be made that the network-cable cross-ownership ban prevents concentration in local video markets. Even if one conceded the existence of such unspecified markets, a rule that prevented ABC, CBS, and NBC—and only those three networks—from owning cable systems—and only cable systems—would strike an efficient competitive balance in the video market only by happenstance.

A third explanation for the rule is that the cable ownership ban is designed to prevent ABC, CBS, and NBC from retarding additional networks, cable or conventional, by excluding these fledgling competitors from network-owned cable systems. This explanation also lacks any empirical or theoretical support. Whatever the state of knowledge in 1970, we now have substantial experience with firms that own both cable program networks and many cable systems. Almost uniformly, these firms do not in fact refuse to carry, on their cable systems, cable networks that compete directly with their program arms.[14]

Of course, this evidence is not directly to the point. The three dominant, conventional networks might behave differently. Two considerations, however, suggest they would not. First, keeping rival networks off one cable system in one market cannot seriously disadvantage that rival in the national market in which networks compete. Thus ABC, CBS, and NBC would have to acquire market power, individually or collectively, over cable system operation nationally before they had the ability to harm competing networks by exclusion. Second, because antitrust laws would prevent any single firm from acquiring such market power, the dominant networks could only do so collectively. In that case they would face all the difficulties of coordinating, covertly and implicitly, their exclusionary behavior described in chapter 6. Finally, if only because none of these firms now owns any cable system, the chance that they could acquire and exercise collective exclusionary power in the future is remote.

In sum, no apparent basis exists for the FCC's across-the-board ban on cable system acquisition by ABC, CBS, and NBC. Such a rule is, at best, a crude method of vindicating the true public concern: preventing any firm from acquiring market power in local or national video markets or in cable system ownership nationwide.

General Principles

The foregoing discussion treats only the specific rules presently enforced by the FCC. That analysis, however, reveals three general principles that should guide regulation of ownership of any local outlet by any network.

First, no identifiable public interest would be served by a complete ban on network ownership of local outlets, whether these outlets employ the same technology as the outlets the networks interconnect (e.g., ABC owning a VHF station or Time, Inc. owning a cable system) or a different technology (e.g., CBS owning a cable system or the Cable News Network owning a UHF station). Indeed, such broad proscriptions may disserve the interest in competition by reducing competition for control of these outlets and by frustrating efficiencies that might be realized by vertical integration.

Second, the public interest does require that, as far as possible, no firm should be permitted to obtain market power within local video markets. Enforcement of that principle would yield the additional benefit of preventing networks from gaining control of sufficient local outlets, in sufficient local markets, to be able to exclude rival networks. Such a rule, or rules, cannot be specified more precisely until the question of how to measure video market concentration is resolved. That question is too complex to answer here. Its complexity cannot, however, justify the FCC's present simplistic prohibitions on local market ownership. These rules fail to account for differences in the number and size of outlets in different markets and neglect to treat conventional network contract affiliation as the rough equivalent of ownership.

A third principle is that no firm, including a network firm, should be permitted to acquire market power within a national video market. Again, the difficult problem arises of how to define such a market or markets. Indeed, the very concept of a national market in this industry is elusive at best. Because viewing choices are made locally, and advertisers seek to reach viewers, the notion that a national video market exists, apart from a series of local markets or a national advertising market, may be incorrect. Until some plausible attempt is made to document and define the existence of one or more national video markets, no nationwide limitation on the number of outlets any firm may acquire can be assessed rationally.

Looked at from the single perspective of the isssue of network regulation, with which this volume deals, these principles yield a simple conclusion. Except for the need to account, in local markets, for conventional network affiliation agreements as well as outright ownership, no public policy is furthered by subjecting network ownership of outlets to any rule different from that applied to all firms generally. ABC and Time, Inc., for example, should be equally free to compete for local outlets, subject to the constraint that neither may acquire market power, nationally or locally.

Network Ownership of Program Supply

Suppose a network decides to integrate vertically "upstream," to program supply, rather than "downstream," to the operation of a local outlet. The analysis is somewhat different because of two characteristics that distinguish program supply.

First, unlike local outlets, whose numbers are closely restricted by FCC policies, program suppliers operate in an industry devoid of any ascertainable barriers to legal or economic entry. No one needs a government license to produce programs. Nor is any substantial capital required since all the equipment can be rented and most of the talent is available to work on a per-program or per-series basis. That program supply could be monopolized, except perhaps in one or two discrete subcategories of programs discussed below, is virtually unthinkable.

Another distinguishing characteristic between network acquisition of stations and of programs is that the latter has a greater self-evident capacity to generate substantial efficiencies. As explained in chapter 7, marrying the network's experience in predicting audience and advertiser tastes with the supplier's skills in assembling programs may greatly reduce the risk of failure. Further, such a combination could diminish the "moral hazard" that a producer may not put forth its best efforts to expend production funds most efficiently. Indeed, the practical reality is that at least the dominant conventional networks are in fact integrated with program suppliers, in particular ventures, to take advantage of these efficiencies. Although most television network series are produced by independent firms pursuant to a contract, those contracts usually give the network extensive control over scripts, casting, and production techniques, and networks exercise that control freely.

For these reasons, formal network integration into program supply is unlikely to affect competition or diversity adversely. To the extent that a change in ownership occurs, that change is likely to be more formal than real. Further, substantial cost-reducing efficiencies may be realized while competitive entry remains unimpeded. Nevertheless, in the past decade producers have virtually besieged public officials with pleas to prevent network integration into program supply. With some minor qualifications, these pleas advance purely private, not public, interests.

Network In-house Production

When it was filed, the apparent principal purpose of the Department of Justice's antitrust suit against ABC, CBS, and NBC was to prevent these networks from producing entertainment programs for themselves. We have been unable to discover a single instance in which any Justice Department or FCC official has suggested that any other network should be so inhibited. Accordingly, we can address only the three evils that in-house production by the dominant three networks are said to produce. Because none of these claims raises an assertion of harm to the public interest, it follows that no other network should be forbidden to produce its programs, either.

First, critics contend that networks may favor in-house programs over independently produced programs. There is simply no conceivable reason why the networks should do this. ABC, CBS, and NBC—like major independent suppliers such as Columbia (owned by Coca-Cola), Paramount (a Gulf and Western subsidiary) and MCA/Universal—are conglomerates or subsidiaries of conglomerates whose goal is to make profits, not programs. If a network can produce in-house at lower cost a program that is as valuable as a program available from an independent supplier, it will undoubtedly do so. But the reverse is equally true. When all other things are equal, networks favor lower costs, not in-house or independent production.

Moreover, even if the contention of favoritism were plausible, it does not bear on the public interest. Public officials have no reason to fear favoritism unless some public policy is disserved by reliance on the disfavored characteristic. For example, networks consistently favor color programs over black-and-white programs. Such discrimination disserves no public policy and so is not objectionable. Similarly, given the system of developing network programs, viewers are unaffected by whether the production company has a contract with, or is owned by, the network.

A second objection, allied to the first, might be that networks may favor in-house production in order to preclude existing or potential rival networks. But this cannot be true. If anything, in-house production frees up independent production resources for which rival networks may bid. If the dominant networks could raise rivals' costs by engaging in in-house production, we might expect them to do so. In fact, the vast bulk of all network entertainment programming is acquired from independent suppliers, a pattern that existed before the Department of Justice suit was commenced.

The Justice Department advanced a third contention, that the networks might employ the fact or the threat of in-house production to obtain lower prices from independent suppliers. Of course, barring resort to illegal violence, no one can make any firm supply programs at unprofitable prices. Thus this contention, if factually accurate, is simply an assertion that networks should receive less, and suppliers more, of the profits gained from program production. Suppliers, advancing their private interests, should and do believe this assertion devoutly. No public interest is affected by the division of these profits, however, so no conscientious regulator should care whether networks do obtain lower prices by threatening in-house production or, if so, how much producers' profits would decline as a result.

Network Purchase of Independent Suppliers

Networks have rarely, if ever, acquired an independent supplier. Nevertheless, the phenomenon could arise and the previous analysis provides ascertainable guidelines for regulators.

Again, the acquisition could harm the public interest if it enabled the network to preclude or hinder entry by rivals, thus diminishing competition among networks and undermining the values of diversity and localism. Unlike the results of network internal expansion into in-house production, acquisition of a program supplier would not increase the program supply resources available to new networks. Further, unlike the effects of exclusivity clauses in program supply contracts, network merger with a supplier would enable the network to deny all the supplier's programs to rival networks.

Despite these more drastic consequences, the fact remains that three conditions would usually be present in any such case, any of which would be sufficient to prevent competitive harm. First, entry into program supply remains easy, so that a new firm could be created easily. Second, production talent—actors, writers, and directors—is not usually tied by long-term contracts to specific firms, so entry along the same lines as the acquired firm should be easy. Third, even barring entry, the merger will not reduce the program supply available to other networks. To the extent that the acquiring network increases its utilization of the acquired supplier, the resources of those suppliers with which the network formerly dealt will be freed up for other networks.

Thus competitors of the acquiring network should be no worse off than they were before the merger. Because the merger is likely to produce efficiencies as well, there should be no reason to contest it. Conversely, if none of the three conditions described above is present, and the supplier's programs are important aspects of network schedules, the merger may be presumptively unlawful. For example, although these conditions almost certainly prevail in entertainment programming, they may not with respect to professional sports. Entry may be difficult because leagues receive governmental insulation from competition and have captured most large markets. Players may be tied to existing leagues and teams by long-term contracts. If other sports or nonsports programming is not a good substitute for the league's games, the acquisition by a network of a league may not eventually free up alternative resources. In short, were ABC to acquire the National Football League, a detailed analysis of possible foreclosure harm would be sensible; if ABC bought Paramount, however, no such fears should arise.

Network Acquisition of Syndication Rights

As discussed above, an FCC rule and a provision of the Department of Justice consent decrees separately prohibit ABC, CBS, and NBC from acquiring syndication rights in network programs. In chapter 8 we considered and rejected each of the arguments for this prohibition that the Commision advanced when it adopted the rule. Now that the FCC has formally proposed to repeal the syndication rule, more sophisticated advocates have stepped forward, advancing a new contention in support of the rule. They argue that the rule usefully prevents networks from disadvantaging their principal competitiors, independent stations, by controlling the market for syndicated programs, the fare upon which these stations principally rely in competing with the established networks. For example, should CBS obtain the syndication rights to "M*A*S*H," it is argued, it could then disadvantage independent stations by refusing to sell them "M*A*S*H" syndication rights.

No evidence of which we are aware confirms or denies the premise of this contention: that the networks' gains in increased advertising revenues would exceed their costs of acquiring syndication rights. Certainly neither the Commission nor the Justice Department ever made such a contention, much less assembled any evidence that it was true. Nor has anyone carefully inquired whether the extraordinary amount of off-network syndicated programming not controlled by the networks would doom such a strategy of monopolization from the outset. Consequently, the regulator must determine the relative merits of either repealing the rule (and running the risk that the asserted network predation will occur) or retaining the rule (and assuming the cost of enforcement and saddling the program supply process with the inefficiencies the rule generates). Several reasons suggest that repeal remains the preferable course.

First, if networks could harm independents in this fashion, they would do so principally through the enforcement of exclusivity clauses, not the acquisition of syndication rights. The exclusivity clause, which may keep a program like "M*A*S*H" out of syndication as long as it remains in first-run production, can deny independents programs when they are much fresher and direct competitors of network fare. Yet these clauses, where employed, are so obviously efficient (as described in chapter 7) that they cannot be abolished. To forbid networks to acquire syndication rights, in order to avoid predatory tactics directed at independent stations, while networks continue to obtain exclusivity, is thus akin to forbidding Mickey Mantle to hit a ball with a flyswatter but allowing him to bat with a Louisville Slugger.

Moreover, these exclusivity clauses have not in fact proved capable of denying independents access to series while those series were still being produced for the network. "M*A*S*H," to extend the example, was in syndication, often on independent stations, during the last three years of its network run. Because acquiring and withholding syndication rights is less harmful to independents than acquiring and enforcing exclusivity clauses, it is thus hard to believe that networks will in fact behave predatorily respecting syndication when they apparently have not done so with regard to exclusivity clauses.

Second, for the reason explained in chapter 2, as network entry barriers are eroded, ABC, CBS, and NBC will increasingly face competition principally from other networks, not from independent stations. In such a case, these networks would gain little or nothing by disadvantaging independent stations while passing up revenues from syndication sales and absorbing the costs of acquiring syndication rights, especially since the "gains" of this behavior would be shared with many other networks, not only two. Proponents of the rule are, in this sense, blinded by the past. They foresee the competitive network environment of the 1990s as akin to that of the 1960s. As explained in chapter 2, that view is an enormous misperception.

Third, networks are unlikely to be able to employ syndication rights to disadvantage independent stations because to do so would require extensive nondetectable collusion. A network adopting such a strategy alone would bear its entire costs, while sharing its benefits with the others. Were CBS to withhold "M*A*S*H," for example, it would bear all those costs while NBC reaped many benefits. Thus only a coordinated policy could be effective, but the requirements of such a policy would be formidable. The networks would have to coordinate their activities so that each always knew which network was to acquire what kinds of syndication rights in which programs, and which network was to pass up what syndication revenues on which program that was to be denied to what independent station. Even if such an agreement could be reached and shielded from discovery by antitrust authorities, each network would immediately develop an incentive to breach the accord, hoping that it could obtain syndication revenues to recoup its expenses in acquiring syndication rights while the others would bear the costs of predation. Of course, each network would also know that all the others had such an incentive, too.

At the very least, these practical problems of coordinating collusive predation dictate that, as network entry increases, the predation rationale for the syndication rule becomes, quite simply, incredible. Once again, the argument rests on a view of television network competition that looks backward, not forward. Indeed, the presumption that independent stations have access to high-quality (high-cost) programming only through the purchase of network reruns is rapidly becoming anachronistic. Some series orginally produced for cable viewers (e.g., "Bizarre") are now beginning to find their way into the rerun market. Other programs that originally appeared on the networks and then were canceled (e.g., "Fame", "Too Close for Comfort") continue to exhibit new episodes on independent stations. If ever the syndication rule served some credible policy purpose, that time is surely past.

Moreover, even in a confined environment, in which only three networks can and do compete, only two practical methods of joint, nonovert collusion to harm independents seem possible. One is for all three networks to refuse to sell any syndication rights they acquire. The other is for each uniformly to discriminate in selling them in favor of its own affiliates. Both strategies if implemented, would be easily detectable.

For these reasons, the balance seems to be clearly in favor of repeal of the rule. If the rule is abolished, the risk is remote that networks will acquire syndication rights to disadvantage independent stations, and if the risk nevertheless materializes, it can be quickly detected and remedied. If the rule is retained, it will continue to pose an obstacle to the efficient allocation of risk between supplier and network. In any event, as new network entry continues, the already slim argument for the rule must necessarily vanish altogether. Even advocates for retaining the rule appear to agree on this point.

Network Operations

Only one federal regulation, the FCC's "dual network" prohibition, controls the extent to which any one firm may engage in networking activities. That rule is easily comprehended and, presumably, easily enforced. But this simplicity is purchased at the price of rationality.

Consider three illustrative applications. One effect of the rule is to ban the merger of any two of the three dominant conventional networks. That result seems quite sensible, at least at the present time, given the power each of these firms exerts and those barriers to new broadcast network entry that are not yet eroded.

A second effect of the dual network rule is to forbid any network that at present interconnects as few as two stations from creating an additional, simultaneously available network. Such a result appears unwarranted, as this hypothetical situation, which alone has been sufficient to trigger the rule, does not suggest any obvious harm to any identifiable public interest. Indeed, this aspect of the rule may hinder achievement of the goals of competition and diversity. Existing networks may be able to realize economies by means of internal expansion that are unavailable to new entrants. For example, program production or audience research costs may be spread over the newly created and the established networks. If those economies are sufficient, an additional network might arise only by internal expansion. There is no reason to proscribe such a development in all cases, regardless of network size.

A third example arises from the fact that the rule permits unlimited mergers among video networks as long as only one of them interconnects conventional television broadcast stations. Thus the rule would not prevent NBC from acquiring the three largest cable networks. In certain circumstances perhaps such a merger should be permisssible. But to permit all such mergers routinely is no more justifiable than routinely to ban all internal expansion of small conventional networks (second hypothesis, above).

If the dual network rule is intolerably simplistic, is there any preferable approach? Certainly a sensible method can be adopted, but it cannot be so easy. To devise an approach capable of yielding consistent, defensible results, one must start with the premise that networks should not be permitted to acquire market power that is unnecessary to realize substantial economies. To implement that premise, however, requires that one define the total amount of networking activity that does not confer market power or is unavoidable because of entry barriers at other levels, principally that of local outlets. This task cannot be accomplished until the difficult problem, described above, of defining the video marketplace is resolved. That problem has only recently begun to be addressed because in the past the FCC has been content to avoid it by promulgating simple numerical ownership limits, such as the dual network and one-to-a-market rules.

But the Commission has avoided confronting the problem of defining the economic markets in which networks operate. A present-day commissioner could justify retaining the dual network rule only by assuming that no more than three networks can exist, so the only issue is whether to prevent their merger. Were the assumption correct, the conclusion would be irresistible.

More than three networks now exist, however, and many more may exist if the Commission continues to relax the entry barriers it has imposed. When the FCC realized these conditions existed in the radio industry, it repealed the ban on dual radio networks, committing itself to apply a more sensitive measure of market power in the future should the need arise. Television is overdue for similar treatment.

Conclusions

Undoubtedly, federal regulation of commercial television network firm size and structure is in the public interest. The goals of competition, diversity and localism are all served by effective prohibitions on network acquisition of monopoly power or the ability to exclude rivals. These goals will usually be achieved by applying antimonopoly policies to all firms, network and nonnetwork alike.

Appropriate regulatory policy, however, may include some specific provisions aimed solely at networks. For example, prohibiting of at least some potential mergers among networks is warranted. In addition, networks may justifiably be forbidden to acquire a program supplier that has substantial market power protected by entry barriers, controls the talent used to produce programs, and provides unique programming that is important to network financial success. Further, although all firms should be forbidden to gain undue control of local markets through acquisition of local broadcast outlets, networks may be specially treated by such a rule in that conventional affiliation agreements may be considered the equivalent of ownership.

Notwithstanding the need for some special treatment of networks, however, the gap is quite large between existing rules and defensible policies designed to further the public interest. Measured by the criteria of the goals of competition, localism and diversity, the ban on network acquisition of syndication rights, the network-cable cross-ownership prohibition, the restriction on dual networking, and the simple numerical limits on station ownership fare very badly. All should be repealed.

Some of the underlying defects in these rules are identical to those infecting regulations of network-affiliate and network-program supply contracts. For example, when defended as an ownership limit, the syndication rule, like so many of the network-affiliate rules, neglects to consider whether the regulated practice is in fact likely to cause the feared injury. The Department of Justice's defense of the limits on in-house production, like the FCC's defense of the financial interest rule, rests upon an ill-conceived notion of what constitutes public, rather than private, harm.

These rules also suffer from another failing: the simplistic resolution of complicated issues. Simple numerical limits on the television stations, networks, and cable systems a network may own are largely just that: simple numerical limits, evidently unrelated to any defined policy of avoiding undue concentration while preserving competition and efficiency. All that can be said for these rules is that they are easy to administer and can be applied without detailed factual investigation. In truth, no more need be said against them. These overly broad proscriptions can prevent activities that serve the public interest, including competition for outlets and efficient network operations. That these public sacrifices might be justified as serving administrators' convenience is, at best, ironic.

These rules appear to manifest a cavalier attitude toward network regulation: if the job is not sufficiently easy to do quickly and correctly, it will be done quickly and then forgotten. Time will expose this flaw. As with the other television network regulations we have studied, these ownership restrictions will also require reexamination, whether it suits the Commission's convenience or not, as legal, technological, and economic barriers to video networks continue to erode. The principles elaborated in this chapter will provide a more enduring substitute, although they will require more detailed factual inquiries to resolve specific cases.

10   Conclusions

Why Regulation of Commercial Television Network
Practices and Structure Deserves Study

Television networks, in one form or another, have dominated the home entertainment medium from its inception and will continue to do so for the foreseeable future.[1] This dominance results chiefly from the extraordinary economies of scale that networking achieves. Once a program is produced for viewers in one city, televising it elsewhere involves only the additional costs of distribution. Nationally distributed television programs, then, can be produced more expensively per program, yet less expensively per viewer, than similar types of programs not as widely distributed.

Moreover, networks that operate throughout the broadcast day and during most days of the year enjoy substantial economies not available to networks that broadcast infrequently. These economies include lower distribution costs, lower transactions costs between network and advertisers and network and local outlets, and a greater ability to spread the risks of program development over a broad range of programs.

Therefore, for good or ill, we must expect that the performance of full-scale, interconnected television networks will be the principal determinant of the amount of satisfaction the American public gains from television for at least the next quarter century. Certainly this has been true for more than the past twenty-five years. For this reason alone, regulatory policy toward commercial television networks must be assigned a very high priority in any overall national communications policy. Indeed, from the viewer's standpoint, regulation of television is regulation of networks.

163

A further reason for carefully examining federal regulation of commercial television network practices at this time is the very recent emergence of a substantial number of new commercial television networks. Many of them employ the still nascent technologies of transmitting television to the home via cable, microwave, or videocassette. Satellite broadcasting networks should emerge within five years. Several adopt the method of charging viewers directly for programs rather than relying on advertiser support. All have the potential to alter radically the range of choices available to network viewers.

These develoments substantially affect analysis of present network regulatory policy in two ways. First, one is forced to confront the question whether those policies themselves could restrict the increase in competition these networks promise, by restricting their entry. Second, we must ask whether these policies are adequate to protect against the possibility that the three dominant, conventional networks (ABC, CBS, and NBC), singly or collectively, might employ practices that entrench their own power or otherwise retard the entry of these new rivals.

Fundamental Issues the Study Must Address

Our study reveals that the central issue in evaluating regulation of network business practices and structure is determining the criteria by which to assess competing policy suggestions.[2] No one can claim infallability on that issue, for, given the peculiar properties of television programs as "public goods," no generally accepted norm provides a simple or observable measure of the desirability of any effects a regulation achieves. But while the issue of which criteria to employ cannot be resolved definitively, one should not be allowed to wish it away. That values and goals may be debatable does not mean they should not be debated or that policymakers should be permitted to resolve questions of such public importance by recourse to intuitive hunches or by comparing the relative elegance of the arguments provided by proponents of private interests.

We conclude that a system characterized by competition among as many outlets as viewers and advertisers are willing to pay for and which are dependent for their success on the attentiveness of viewers is and should be the paramount goal of this aspect of U.S. communications policy. This goal, an amalgam of the values of competition, diversity, and localism, seems to comport most closely with First Amendment principles, fundamental national economic regulatory policy, and the Communications Act of 1934, the charter of the F.C.C. It appears, moreover, to reflect the same approach U.S. regulatory policy takes toward other mass media such as newspapers, magazines, movies, and live theater.

This choice of goals not only affirms certain values, but explicitly rejects others. For example, our criteria mean that the desirability of a network regulation is not to be measured by its effects on the relative profits of industry members. Nor should we care whether the policy promotes or retards the viability of networking as compared to other methods of financing or distributing television programs. Nor would we applaud a regulation designed to change the content of programs viewers would otherwise choose; our criteria imply that viewers should obtain what they, not we or the FCC, desire.

The present study reveals another fundamental issue, hidden below the surface of network regulation, and, in our experience, not often discussed. That issue is what the "network" in "network regulation" means. More specifically, is the question regulators confront how best to superintend the structure and behavior of ABC, CBS, and NBC, or is it, rather, how best to lay down rules for conducting the business of television networking (given, of course, the historic dominance of the major three)? Our study insists that regulators address the latter question.

ABC, CBS, and NBC achieved their dominance not because any law of physics or Platonic beatitude dictates that three is precisely the "right" number of networks. Rather, a confluence of avoidable FCC policy choice—especially those allocating the VHF and UHF spectrum and others designed to block the growth of pay and cable television—virtually assured that only three national, full-scale television networks would succeed.[3] The FCC has abandoned or mitigated these policies in the past five years, and thus to assume that only three networks will dominate in the future is, at best, hazardous. Certainly policies designed to be viable a decade hence must not rest exclusively on the assumption that only three full-scale networks will exist.

A Coherent Regulatory Policy toward Commercial
Television Networks

In light of the preceding argument, one can describe a coherent system of network regulation once the function of networks is understood. Television networks act as middlemen, drawing together advertisers, viewers, program suppliers and local outlets to achieve the significant scale economies described above. Wherever these four groups exist in sufficient numbers, a network can arise to serve them. Thus a network can achieve market power, which would enable it to enact in an anticompetitive fashion or to restrict the viability of local outlets or to refuse to serve viewers' tastes, only by monopolizing one or more of these groups or by merger or agreement with other networks.

It is inconceivable that any network could acquire control, by contract or merger, over enough viewers or advertisers to alter the opportunities available to other networks (except, of course, by offering more attractive programs). Thus regulatory policy must consider the extent to which networks may acquire control over (1) other networks, (2) program suppliers, and (3) local outlets.

Interaction among networks may be handled by the straightforward application of antitrust policy, as applied to business firms generally.[4] Independent networks should not be allowed to agree among themselves on the terms on which, or the markets in which, they buy or sell programs, nor on the types of programs they offer. Networks should not be permitted to merge or engage in joint ventures where the merger or venture would give the resulting firm market power or would make collusion among networks substantially easier. Nor should any network be permitted, by internal expansion, to develop so many networks that it obtains market power, unless that position is achieved by superior skill, foresight, and industry.

To the reader not versed in antitrust law, some of the terms used above will undoubtedly appear imprecise. In truth, these phrases describe the common approaches underlying cases spanning almost a century of antitrust enforcement and can be applied concretely with reference to those cases. The real difficulty here is describing how market power should be measured in the specific business of networking. To date, the FCC has been content with a simple (indeed, so simple as to be indefensible) ban on operating two conventional networks simultaneously in the same local markets.

Regulation of network dealings with program suppliers[5] and with local affiliated outlets[6] must proceed from certain principles that one would call obvious had the FCC and Justice Department not overlooked them so frequently. In both cases, the arrangements between the parties (network-program supplier and network-affiliate) are alike in four respects.

First, both parties' interests are usually congruent, not divergent. That is, in each case the two firms have an overriding incentive to maximize the joint profits that accrue from networking. Their interests usually diverge only in how those profits are to be divided.

Second, in neither case does a network have the incentive or ability to harm the other firm by coercing it to engage in unprofitable activities. A program supplier will not produce a network program that the supplier believes would reduce its profits. An affiliate will not clear a network program if that clearance will reduce its profitability.

Third, when the FCC or the Justice Department regulates one term of a complex program supply or affiliation agreement, in order to affect the production or clearance question or to redistribute profits, the network almost always has available other terms that may be altered to escape the regulation's intended effect.

Fourth, both the program supply and the affiliation contract will necessarily contain terms that "disadvantage" other networks. For example, if a network obtains exclusive rights to "My Mother the Car," no other network can broadcast it; if it acquires an option on an affiliate's time, exercise of that option will exclude other networks from that time. However, these terms usually appear upon inspection to have the additional consequence of reducing the costs of networking. Regulators must choose whether to ban or regulate such terms to avoid exclusionary behavior or to permit them in order to foster efficient competition.

Several factors counsel permissiveness. (1) These terms cannot be exclusionary in an environment where many rival networks operate. The price of obtaining these terms would exceed their value unless they lowered costs. (2) In a system of only three networks, but where entry is blockaded by federal regulation, there is no need to employ these terms unless they are efficient. Thus the fact that exhibition exclusivity and time optioning existed in the 1950s and 1960s can be cited as evidence that they serve in some measure to reduce costs. (3) For three networks simultaneously to employ such contract terms in exclusionary fashion would require implicit or explicit agreement on which network or networks would pay which costs. Further, the gains from the exclusion would have to be shared with (indeed, might well be largely captured by) the program suppliers and affiliates, and networks would have to agree on these sharing arrangements. (4) No technique exists for determining objectively the precise point at which a particular provision is no longer entirely justified by efficiency needs and serves only to exclude. In principle, a four-year exclusivity provision may represent, as it were, three years for cost reduction and one for excluding rivals; in practice, no regulator can tell.

In one important respect, the network-affiliate and network-program supplier relationships differ with respect to a fundamental principle. Entry into program supply is very easy; entry into providing television signals to homes was, until very recently, virtually blockaded and remains impeded by government regulation and, ultimately, by technical spectrum utilization considerations.

If all the foregoing is taken into account, straightforward policy proscriptions can be developed. In both cases it is far wiser to avoid detailed contract regulation until some identifiable evidence of exclusionary effects arises. The recent erosion of governmental entry barriers to networking means that regulators should not have to guess at the effects of a contract clause on network entry, but can observe the behavior of many networks with respect to it.

Moreover, the dominant networks probably can be prevented from precluding competition for other networks simply by denying them control over key suppliers or affiliates.[7] In the case of affiliation , this means prohibiting multiple affiliations (including ownership) that give a network power within a local market. In the case of program supply, this means preventing one network from acquiring a supplier (by merger or by long-term contract) for that network's exclusive use if the acquired firm itself produces a unique product that others cannot approximate and that is important to the success of networks. Given the ease with which firms may enter the program supply industry, this test will be met rarely, if ever. Some suppliers, however, such as professional sports leagues, may prove upon close inspection to be insulated by governmental protections from effective competition and may also be seen to provide programs important to networks' success. If so, the acquisition of such a supplier by a network should be carefully examined, although the first option to pursue is eradication of the supplier's governmental protection.

Principal Criticisms

Critical Evaluation of Present Policies

A major conclusion of the present study is that a brief and simple set of network television regulatory policies is called for, once we understand that the first priority is to continue to reduce as far as possible entry barriers to networking. The second major conclusion is that the system advocated here differs radically from the one now in place. Of the FCC's rules, we would retain only two (both of which are incidental to the main issue discussed here).[8] We would accept none of the countless regulations on program supply contracts imposed by the Department of Justice consent decree. And the FCC has on its books none of the regulatory policies we propose, although conceivably the Commission or the Department of Justice could apply similar policies by subjecting the networks to traditional antitrust rules.

The question remains, then, Why do we reject so harshly the present system? How have the FCC and Department of Justice, in our view, erred? Our analysis suggests that these regulators have made five types of errors, the avoidance of which would have have produced a system of regulation like that advocated here:

1. Creating Problems Where None Exist.

FCC regulations of the network-program supply process rest, at least in part, on the assumption that the rules are necessary to compensate suppliers for economic losses inflicted by the network. The Justice Department consent decree also seems to rest on this premise. Not only is the public interest unaffected by the relative profitability of these firms, there is also no reason to believe that program suppliers do not expect to earn a profit on their network dealings or that networks could induce them to produce programs in the expectation of losing money. The ostensible problem simply does not exist.

Similarly, regulation of the degree of graduation in network-affiliate compensation plans appears to rest, in part, on the view that graduated payments enable the network to purchase affiliates' clearances more cheaply. In fact, networks cannot induce stations to clear unprofitable programs, and the chief effect of graduated compensation is to separate the issue of what programs to clear from the issue of how large a percentage of networking profits will be returned to affiliates. The latter issue is resolved by the relative bargaining power of the network and its affiliate, not by the manner in which the duty to compensate is set.

2. Devising Unresponsive Solutions to Real Problems

FCC regulations of the network-affiliate contract are defended largely on the grounds that these rules are necessary to prevent foreclosure of other networks. Certainly ABC, CBS, and NBC have incentives to foreclose rivals, if the gains from foreclosure exceed its cost. In fact, however, it is quite unlikely that the regulated affiliation practices would be useful to a successful, profitable practice of exclusion. Indeed, so long as multiple affiliations (including affiliation by ownership) in key markets are forbidden, the dominant networks can obtain no advantage over other full-scale networks by terms of affiliation agreements. And the economics of full-scale networking provide ABC, CBS, and NBC sufficient advantages over less fully developed networks that we cannot expect restrictive affiliation clauses to be worth their costs if they serve only to exclude such competition.

3. Imposing Unworkable Solutions

Whether the problem is real or imaginary, the FCC has exhibited a remarkably consistent propensity for devising solutions that do not work. If program producers are undercompensated, forbidding network acquisition of syndication rights will not change that fact. Networks will simply reduce the license fee they offer for programs, or alter some other contract term, to reflect the program's reduced value to the network.

If the goal of forbidding option time is to prevent networks from foreclosing local outlets to other networks or to nonnetwork sources, that rule will not work. Networks remain free to structure other terms of the affiliation contract in order to effect the carriage of network programs. For example, they may increase the degree of compensation graduation or vary the advertising time available for sale by stations within or adjacent to network programs. Although these responses are imperfect in that they do not prevent network profits from declining, they are often sufficient to prevent the Commission's goals from being achieved.

These and other similar solutions are flawed because they treat the manifestations rather than the sources of network bargaining or market power. Having been forbidden to achieve their objectives in one manner, networks may be expected to seek other means to the same end. Unless the regulation strikes directly at the acquisition of bargaining or market power, the networks will be able to exert that power through other methods. Because ABC, CBS, and NBC owe their power to governmentally imposed entry barriers and unavoidable economies of scale, alteration of terms in program supply or affiliation contracts will not affect their ability to benefit from exercising that power.

4. Treating Administrative Convenience as a Primary Goal

As we observed in chapter 9, the FCC's ownership policies can be understood most charitably as the results of a choice not to confront the difficult task of determining how to measure market power in the television industry. The simplistic prohibitions on network ownership of a single cable system (coexisting with a seven-station limit on network ownership of conventional television stations) or of two networks (but only where the networks operate simultaneously, in the same markets, and through VHF or UHF stations) are utterly unrelated to any specific goal of network regulation that we or the Commission have advanced.

5. *Thinking Small*

The most egregious and persistent error of federal policy to date, in our judgment, has been the practice of approaching network regulation with blinders on. This practice has taken two forms. First, the Commission, as far as we can ascertain, has never asked whether it might be better able to achieve its goal by reducing network entry barriers rather than by regulating the commercial practices of networks. None of the FCC's principal network regulations would be imposed on a system in which network entry was relatively free, as witnessed by the Commission's removal of those rules from radio networks. Yet the FCC has never asked whether a proposed television network regulation should be rejected in favor of pursuing a policy of reducing network entry barriers. Indeed, at the conclusion of its studies of network practices in 1959 and again in 1970, the Commission promulgated additional network regulations, justified as useful means to promote network competition, and almost at the same time adopted a series of rules designed to block or severely limit the growth of cable television networks.[9] By 1977, when the latest Network Inquiry was launched, the FCC's views on these questions had not changed. Apparently, the Commission was utterly oblivious to the central fact that nothing affects the nature and extent of network competition, program diversity, and local viewer control as much as the number of outlets available in local markets.

The Commission's other way of thinking small has been to draft policies designed to protect nonnetwork sources from network competition. Thus a purpose of banning option time was to spur the growth of nonnetwork programs, and the 1970 program supply rules were supposed to stimulate the first-run syndication business. At best, such policies disserve the public interest by attaching a specific preference to nonnetwork fare. At worst, they are ineffective because they are unworkable. In truth, they not only deflect resources from the larger issues the Commission should confront, but also impose inefficient practices on networks subject to the rules.

Occasionally, in a grand gesture of futility and obfuscation reminiscent of the 1962 New York Mets or a Spike Jones rendition of *The Pines of Rome*, the FCC manages to commit all five types of errors at once. Just such an occasion produced the Prime Time Access Rule.

PTAR was said to cure the problem that network affiliates do not exercise discretion in choosing what to broadcast during prime time. In fact affiliates make very deliberate choices to affiliate and to clear network programs (error 1).

The rule was said to avoid subjecting viewers to a limited choice of programs, all of which had been found acceptable to one of only three firms. By substituting three affiliates for three networks, the rule does nothing to alleviate this "funnel" effect (error 2).

PTAR, the Commission said, would generate business for first-run syndicators who would then be able to supply prime-time programs as expensively financed as those offered by networks. But the networks can spend more on programming not because they produce for prime time but because they enjoy economies of scale not available to a firm supplying only one program nationwide per week. Accordingly, to our knowledge no program produced for the access period has subsequently been adopted by affiliates as a substitute for clearing a network program during the remainder of prime time (error 3).

The access rule was said to be an experiment, but the Commission has never tested its effects empirically. When confronted with a strong prima facie case that the rule had not produced network quality programs because it could not, the FCC simply invented a new rationale for PTAR—to encourage local programming. The rule contains a definition of covered "networks" that the present FCC concedes was chosen for no apparent reason (error 4).

The asserted purposes of PTAR could have been achieved more easily and effectively by reducing network entry barriers. Instead, the Commission decided to shelter nonnetwork programs from network competition, in the process reducing viewers' and stations' choices and imposing disadvantages on those networks that happen to be subject to the rule without increasing competition among networks one iota (error 5).

Speaking of his Mets in 1962, Casey Stengel reportedly asked, "Can't anyone here play this game?" He might as well have been asking the FCC about network regulation policies when it promulgated the Prime Time Access Rule.

Specific Harms of the Present System

We have criticized present regulatory policies of the FCC and the Department of Justice not only because they are inadequately substantiated, factually and theoretically, but also because these policies have resulted in specific harms to the public interest with regard to competition, diversity, and localism.

First, as has been stated, existing FCC rules have been adopted in lieu of measures that might have contributed directly to these goals. Network regulations have substituted a futile policy of protecting nonnetwork sources from network competition for an attainable policy that would greatly increase competition among networks without reducing any of the opportunities available to nonnetwork fare.

Moreover, these regulations impose inefficient methods of operation on the firms subject to them. Where these firms are fledgling networks, these handicaps might retard the growth they could otherwise achieve as the FCC lifts its own network entry barriers. When these firms are ABC, CBS, and NBC, they are saddled with higher costs for no public purpose. In both cases, because none of the rules applies to firms interconnecting outlets that are not conventional broadcast stations, the rules handicap traditional forms of networks relative to those that employ as affiliates outlets (such as cable or MDS systems) that are not considered broadcast licensees.

Causes of the Present Failures

If our analyses are correct, one might ask how such regulatory failure can be avoided in the future. Can we identify a flaw in the process that would produce such results?

One flaw is evident. Like most of us, regulators are reluctant to take back benefits after granting them, no matter how tentative the original grant may have been. That failing probably explains why the FCC, for so long a period, did not act directly upon network dominance by reducing the entry barriers new networks confronted.

The problem arose in the following manner.[10] Very few television stations came on the air before World War II, and no authorizations were permitted during the war. In 1945 the FCC faced a dilemma: it believed television should ultimately be confined to the UHF spectrum, but it did not want to hold back any longer the pent-up demand for TV service while technical adjustments were made. Consequently, the Commission made some VHF allocations available immediately. By 1948 the FCC knew the geographical allocations adopted in 1945 were unworkable, so it "froze" all pending TV station applications to develop a new allocation plan. The freeze, which was expected to last six months, was lifted in 1952 when the current allocation plan was adopted.

By 1952, 108 VHF stations whose authorizations had been granted before the freeze were on the air. The 1952 allocation plan did not affect a single one of these 108 licensees. Indeed, students of the 1952 plan have argued that the FCC devised its allocation system, in part, to avoid moving the 108 "pioneers." As a result, the framework for the U.S. television system came to limit that system to one containing only three networks.

In subsequent years, the FCC thwarted cable and pay television on the grounds that their development might undermine the television system established by the 1952 plan.[11] By this perverse route, the "temporary" decision of 1945 spawned its own vested interests, and the preservation of the system these interests dictated became the determinant of Commission policy. The viewing public is served by only three conventional television networks and by nonconventional competitors, as yet only fledglings, in order that 108 licensees may retain their "temporary" privileges.

There are precisely 108 reasons, then, why the FCC erected insurmountable barriers to network entry and persisted in maintaining them for so long. And its persistence in repeatedly committing the five types of analytical errors described above led the Commission (and later the Department of Justice) to compound that mistake by erecting a series of regulatory policies toward networks that lacked a coherent rationale or a demonstrable tendency to further the welfare of television viewers.

The FCC acted unwisely, but not atypically, in pursuing a regulatory course that first substituted monopoly for competition and then sought to achieve public interest benefits by means of detailed regulation of firms shielded from marketplace competition. Many other regulatory schemes in the U.S. have been dominated by this schizophrenic approach.

In the telecommunications arena, the FCC for over thirty years believed the fiction that long-distance communications could be provided only under conditions of natural monopoly.[12] This occurred despite the advent of microwave transmission during World War II, which rendered the natural monopoly assumption obsolete. Relying on this assumption, the FCC repeatedly denied requests for entry by new firms. In the process, it created vested interests in maintaining the status quo by fostering subsidization of local service from the profits earned from long-distance operations. Meanwhile the Commission also sought to impose detailed rate and service requirements on AT&T's long-distance service. After thirty years, the FCC finally acknowledged that competition in the provision of long-distance service was not only feasible but in the public interest as well. Still, the Commission made this acknowledgment only grudgingly, spurred by pressure from the courts. It took even longer for the FCC to discover that if local service subsidies were in the public interest, there were other, more efficient methods that could provide the same subsidy.

The experience of the Civil Aeronautics Board presents another case (fortunately now corrected) in point.[13] Having concluded, with little substantive examination, that airline competition would be "destructive," Congress and the CAB sought to limit that competition through entry restrictions. Later rationales provided the CAB with additional support for its restrictive policies, particularly the need to subsidize service to small communities. Having restricted entry, there was still the possibility that airlines in some markets might compete on the basis of price. To restrict that competition and thus preserve the profits necessary to subsidize small community service, the CAB set fares at nearly monopoly levels. Having fixed fares, the CAB found that competition in service quality dissipated the profits that regulated fares and restricted entry were designed to maintain. With service competition, particularly in flight frequency, generating excess aircraft capacity, the CAB further strengthened its entry and fare regulation and encouraged the airlines to form a domestic cartel.

Like the FCC and Department of Justice in their regulation of broadcasting, until recently the CAB never seemed to grasp the underlying economics of the industry and never anticipated the inevitable but obvious consequences of its policies. Put simply, the destructive competition argument was a fiction. It is interesting to note that Congress, in deregulating the airline industry, discovered an alternative to the unworkable entry and fare restrictions to ensure adequate service to small communities—a direct subsidy. Much the same story could be told of Interstate Commerce Commission regulation, with one difference.[14] The saga of the CAB appears to be drawing to a happy close; the end of the ICC tale has yet to be written.

That a series of analytical errors underlies these decisions and that these errors are not entirely unique to network regulation seem clear, but these conclusions remain incomplete. To describe regulators as people who simply engage in disinterested but incorrect analysis is not our purpose. The modern theory of public choice teaches us that regulators, like firms and households, behave purposefully and seek to serve their own interests within the constraints they face.[15] The theory argues that, rather than serving the public interest, regulators serve those interests that are sufficiently large to have a major stake in the political process and are sufficiently cohesive that they can organize for political action. The question that naturally arises is, What are the interests that FCC commissioners seek to serve, and what limitations are there on their behavior? Perhaps, if we could answer that question we could explain why the commissioners have been unconcerned with complaints that their analyses are flawed.

Some of the policies pursued by the Commission seem quite consistent with public choice theory. For example, the various policies designed to benefit affiliates at the expense of the networks may result from the fact that affiliates have sufficiently concentrated interests and yet are sufficiently numerous that they represent a powerful political force. Where FCC policy succeeds in shifting profits from networks to affiliates, it may serve the interests of politicians to support those policies even if the result is to make the viewing public no better off, or even worse off. It is not, of course, that networks are not powerful political actors but that, for many politicians, the support of local broadcasters—in the form of electoral coverage if not outright endorsement—is far more important than is the support of the networks. It is possible, therefore, that FCC policies that seek to benefit affiliates at the expense of the networks can be explained in this manner.

More difficult to explain are Commission policies intended to benefit program producers at the expense of the networks. Although it can be argued that the FCC benefits local broadcast stations because of the political favors they can bestow on incumbent politicians, it is by no means obvious that a similar argument can be made for the Commission's regulation of the network-program supplier relationship. Even if the FCC can shift profits from, say, NBC to MCA—and we have already argued that it is unlikely that the financial interest and syndication rules do so—it is unclear why the Commission should favor such a shift. Surely the interests of producers are not more coherent than those of the networks, and organizing for political action would appear to be more difficult for producers. Nonetheless, the Commission has exhibited an astonishing degree of concern for the interests of producers during the past decade.

Difficult as it may be to explain why the FCC has favored the interests of producers over those of the networks, at least the rules limiting the interests that the networks can acquire in independently produced programs had an identifiable, intended beneficiary. It is virtually impossible, however, using public choice theory, to explain why the Commission adopted rules such as the ban on network ownership of cable television systems at a time when the Commission was severely limiting the growth of cable, and the cable industry was a relatively weak political force. Indeed, one of the arguments advanced by the Commission for the ban was that the networks might employ cable system ownership to limit the growth of this nascent competitor. But since the FCC was simultaneously pursuing a vigorous anticable policy, it is hard to see why the Commission would regard such behavior by the networks as undesirable. Nothing in the theory of public choice prepares us for such a result.

Of course, all of these rules have one thing in common. All are intended to harm the networks.[16] The single theory that is consistent with the adoption of all of these rules is that, in one way or another, they are designed to limit the power of the networks.

As just noted, however, while it adopted a set of policies that were ostensibly aimed at limiting network power, the Commission simultaneously pursued another set of policies that were actually cementing that power. To be sure, the FCC probably did not choose these policies in order to provide benefits to the networks. Their intended beneficiaries were almost certainly the owners of broadcast stations. But they benefited the networks as well because they made it impossible for new broadcast networks to be formed or for networks financed by viewer payments and using alternative delivery systems to come into being.

Therefore, the power of incumbent broadcasters made it difficult for the FCC to adopt policies that would seriously limit the power of the broadcast networks because the only policies that could really have that effect would also have harmed the broadcasters. The result has been a set of makeshift policies which, at best, could have marginally limited network power and, at worst, could have caused the television system to adopt a series of inefficient practices. In fact, probably none of these policies had a serious impact on the industry because if they had they would have imposed significant costs on broadcast station owners as well, and broadcast station owners had no desire to destroy the network system because they were among its beneficiaries. At the same time, they wished to obtain a larger share of the profits generated by the industry, as did independent program producers. The FCC was thus obliged to try to limit network power while not actually harming the network system. But, as could have been guessed, this turned out to be harder to do than the Commission anticipated. Indeed, much of our analysis reveals the persistent attempts, and the consistent failures, of the Commission as it went about trying to limit network power and shift profits to other industry participants, using a set of tools ill-suited to the task.

We are left with an explanation of FCC behavior that leaves us, at least, uncomfortable. Although a good deal of Commission behavior probably stemmed from a desire to protect local broadcasters—even though it produced unintended benefits for the networks—other behavior cannot be so easily explained. There is no satisfactory explanation, at least one based on public choice principles, of the preference for the interests of producers over those of the networks. And it is even more difficult to explain rules like the ban on network-cable crossownership.

Two other possibilities deserve mention, although they are not explanations to which we turn happily. First, one might argue that FCC opposition to the networks was simply part of a general animus toward large institutions. The networks, being the largest, most important, and most powerful institutions in the broadcasting industry are likely to attract the attention of those who wish to place limits on concentrated power. Rules limiting the networks in their dealings with affiliates and program producers can perhaps be explained in this fashion. But this explanation cannot be reconciled with the fact, documented throughout this book, that the net effect of FCC policies has been to entrench, not dissipate, the power of the dominant networks. If opponents of concentrated power were in charge at the Commission, why, one might ask, could they not succeed in striking more effective blows at the sources of that power?

Finally, it is possible that the FCC has always intended to serve the public interest but has failed to analyze correctly the factors that limit the ability of the television system to serve that interest. In this view, bringing better analysts to the Commission is the way to achieve better policy. Since the authors of this book went to the FCC hoping to contribute to improved policy analysis, we cannot dismiss this explanation out of hand. But the persistent failure of the FCC to reach results justifiable under a public interest standard makes it terribly difficult to believe that the agency always tried to meet that standard. With this observation, we have come full circle. We can say confidently only that no theory of regulatory behavior convincingly explains FCC actions toward television networks.

Charting the Future

Fortunately, FCC actions since the mid-1970s virtually assure the ultimate demise of the present regulatory scheme imposed on commercial television networks.[17] Cable, STV, MDS, and DBS have been loosed from their regulatory fetters. The Commission apparently is irreversibly committed to substantial disruption of the 1952 UHF-VHF allocation system by the introduction of low-power television and to permitting pay television and advertiser-supported video to exist side by side. Videocassettes and videodiscs flourish in an unregulated environment.

As these technologies and industries mature, they will provide bases for the establishment of networks that can challenge the dominance of ABC, CBS, and NBC. Moreover, their very existence will undermine whatever surface plausibility surrounds existing regulations. If the Commission does not voluntarily repeal them, as it did for radio networks, then courts will have no choice but to declare them baseless, as occurred with respect to the Commission's rules restricting pay cable.[18]

We know of no way to predict what regulatory policies will supplant the existing system. We believe the system we have described above is fully adequate to whatever particular form of network competition will emerge. But whether this system will be adopted depends, in large measure, on whether a new method of analysis can replace the error-ridden approach that has dominated regulators' decisions to date.

Notes

.

While conducting the FCC's Network Inquiry from 1978 to 1980, we released over 3,000 pages of data and analysis, all of which was distributed for public comment and review before publication in final form, and one concluding report. In writing this book, we have relied heavily on the data contained in those reports. Two books published by the Commission at the conclusion of the Network Inquiry are particularly relevant in this respect. *New Television Networks: Entry, Jurisdiction, Ownership and Regulation, Vol. 1* (FCC, 1980) contains the final report of the Network Inquiry and is cited below as *New Networks 1. New Television Networks: Entry, Jurisdiction, Ownership and Regulation, Vol. 2* (FCC, 1980) contains extensive reports on the history of U.S. commercial radio and television networks, the network-affiliate relationships, and the business of producing, acquiring, and distributing television programs. It is cited below as *New Networks 2.*

Chapter 1

1. See FCC, *Report on Chain Broadcasting* (1941).

2. The first of these studies, completed in 1957, is reprinted in *Report of the House Committee on Interstate and Foreign Commerce*, H.R. Rep. no. 1297, 85th Cong., 2d sess. (1958). The remainder are summarized in FCC, Network Inquiry Special Staff: *A Review of the Proceedings of the Federal Communications Commission Leading to the Adoption of the Prime Time Access Rule, the Financial Interest Rule and the Syndication Rule* (Oct. 1979).

3. See 47 C.F.R. § 73.658 (1983).

4. See *New Networks 2*: 653–716, for descriptions of the history of these lawsuits and the provisions of the consent decrees.

5. *Federal Register*, vol. 42, no. 17, p. 4992 (Jan. 26,1977) (docket no. 21049).

6. T.G. Krattenmaker and A.R. Metzger, "FCC Regulatory Authority over Commercial Television Networks: The Role of Ancillary Jurisdiction," *Northwestern University Law Review* 77 (1982):461–86.

7. *Report, Statement of Policy and Order*, 63 FCC 2d 674 (1977).

Chapter 2

1. *Cable TV Advertising* 4 (Feb. 22, 1984).

2. FCC, *TV Broadcast Financial Data—1980*.

3. Prior to 1957, when DuMont was attempting to establish a network in television's infancy, the situation was more complicated. Occasionally, disaffiliation has occurred in more recent years when more than one affiliate of the same network served one market.

4. *New Networks* 2:420–21.

5. P. A. Samuelson, "The Pure Theory of Public Expenditure," *Review of Economics and Statistics* 36 (1954):387.

6. See FCC, *Report on Chain Broadcasting* (1941).

7. See, e.g., R. E. Park, "New Television Networks: An Update" (printed as an appendix to *New Networks 1*:143, 162–65).

8. See National Cable Television Ass'n, "Satellite Services Report," March 1984.

9. See American Tel. & Tel. Co., Long Lines Dep't., 67 FCC 2d 1134 (1977), reconsid. denied, 70 FCC 2d 2031 (1978), aff'd sub nom., ABC v. FCC, No. 79-1261 (D.C. Cir. 1980). See also Hughes Sports Network, Inc., 25 FCC 2d 560 (1970).

10. See FCC, Network Inquiry Special Staff: *Video Interconnection: Technology, Costs and Regulatory Policy* (March 1980):12–14.

11. See Specialized Common Carrier Services, 29 FCC 2d 870 (1971), aff'd sub nom. Washington Util. & Transportation Comm'n v. FCC, 513 F.2d 1142 (9th Cir.), cert. denied, 423 U.S. 836 (1975); see also MCI Telecommunications Corp. v. FCC, 580 F. 2d 590 (D.C. Cir.), cert. denied, 439 U.S. 980 (1978); MCI Telecommunications Corp. v. FCC, 561 F.2d 365 (D.C. Cir. 1977), cert. denied, 434 U.S. 1040 (1978).

12. See Regulatory Policies Concerning Resale and Shared Use of Common Carrier Services and Facilities, 60 FCC 2d 261 (1976), reconsid., 62 FCC 2d 588 (1977).

13. Ibid., 273–74; 298–99.

14. See American Tel. & Tel. Co., 88 FCC 2d 1656 (1982).

15. See Domestic Communications-Satellites, 35 FCC 2d 844 (1972), reconsid., 38 FCC 2d 665 (1972).

16. See Regulatory Policies Concerning Resale and Shared Use of Common Carrier Services and Facilities, 60 FCC 2d 261, 308–12 (1976), reconsid. 62 FCC 2d 588 (1977). See also Southern Satellite Systems, Inc., 62 FCC 2d 153 (1976); United Video, Inc., 69 FCC 2d 1629 (1978).

17. See Regulation of Domestic Receive-Only Satellite Earth Stations, 74 FCC 2d 205 (1977).

18. See FCC, Network Inquiry Special Staff: *Video Interconnection: Technology, Costs and Regulatory Policy* (March 1980):47; *Cable TV Technology* 1 (July 26, 1983).

19. See, e.g., Second Report and Order, 2 FCC 2d 725 (1966); Report and Order, 36 FCC 2d 141 (1972).

20. See Report and Order, 57 FCC 2d 625 (1976); Report and Order, 79 FCC 2d 663 (1980), aff'd sub. nom. Malrite Television v. FCC, 652 F.2d 1140 (2d Cir.), cert. denied sub. nom. Nat'l Ass'n of Broadcasters v. FCC, 454 U.S. 1143 (1982).

21. See National Cable Television Ass'n, "Satellite Services Report," March 1984.

22. See Fourth Report and Order, 15 FCC 2d 466 (1968), aff'd sub.nom. National Ass'n of Theatre Owners v. FCC, 420 F.2d 194 (D.C. Cir. 1969), cert. denied, 397 U.S. 922 (1970).

23. See Memorandum Opinion and Order, 23 FCC 2d 825 (1970).

24. See Home Box Office v. FCC, 567 F.2d 7 (D.C. Cir.), cert. denied, 434 U.S. 829 (1977).

25. See Report and Order, 42 Rad. Reg. 2d (P&F) 1207 (1978).

26. See National Cable Television Ass'n, "Cable TV Developments" (April 1984), p. 1; National Cable Television Ass'n, "Satellite Services Report" (March 1984).

27. See *Pay TV Newsletter* (Dec. 17, 1983 and Jan. 30, 1984).

28. United States v. Southwestern Cable Co., 392 U.S. 157 (1968).

29. T. L. Schuessler, "Structural Barriers to the Entry of Additional Television Networks: The Federal Communications Commission's Spectrum Management Policies," *Southern California Law Review* 54 (1981):875–1000.

30. See Amendment of section 3.606 of the Commission's Rules and Regulations (Sixth Report and Order), 41 FCC 148 (1952).

31. See *New Networks 1*:65.

32. Ibid., 67.

33. Ibid., 78, 81.

34. Ibid., 68, 78, 81.

35. See First Report and Order, 44 Fed. Reg. 60, 091 (1979).

36. See Third Report and Order, 90 FCC 2d 341 (1982).

37. See Notice of Proposed Rulemaking, 83 FCC 2d 51 (1980). In a separate proceeding in 1980, the Commission authorized a VHF "drop-in" station in four communities. Report and Order, 81 FCC 2d 233 (1980).

38. See Report and Order, 47 Fed. Reg. 21, 468 (1982).

39. Ibid., 21, 474; 21, 487–93.

40. See Third Report and Order, 90 FCC 2d 341 (1982).

41. See Report and Order, 90 FCC 2d 676 (1982).

42. See, e.g., Memorandum Opinion and Order, FCC 82–427 (released Oct. 13, 1982; approving application of Satellite Television Corp., subsidiary of Comsat Corp.).

43. Report and Order, 48 Fed. Reg. 33, 873 (1983) (additional channels) and Further Notice of Proposed Rulemaking, 48 Fed. Reg. 49, 309 (1983) (lottery).

Chapter 3

1. See, e.g., P. A. Samuelson, "The Pure Theory of Public Expenditure," *Review of Economics and Statistics* 36 (1954):387.

2. Another way to express this point is that if programs are financed by advertising revenues, most viewers will have access to television programs at zero marginal cost but the programs aired will reflect the number of people (or the number of types of people advertisers value) who watch those programs, not the value people place on the programs.

3. Thus neither a pay-program nor an advertiser-supported system is "perfect" in yielding viewer satisfaction. The question we address in this study, then, is whether existing or proposed regulations tend to make viewers generally better off than they would be in the absence of regulation.

4. 47 U.S.C. § 303 (1976).

5. T. G. Krattenmaker and A. R. Metzger, "FCC Regulatory Authority over Commercial Television Networks: The Role of Ancillary Jurisdiction," *Northwestern University Law Review* 77 (1982):403.

6. 47 U.S.C. § 326 (1976).

7. See, e.g., CBS v. DNC, 412 U.S. 94, 116–17 (1973).

8. See, e.g., FCC v. Sanders Bros. Radio Station, 309 U.S. 470 (1940); NBC v. United States, 319 U.S. 190 (1943).

9. Although, of course, viewers' preferences may be counted in less than perfectly desirable ways. See the hypothetical discussion of the advertiser-supported system and "Gilligan's Island" in the text at n. 3 above.

10. To be complete, we should note another theoretical difficulty, beyond that springing from the "public good" problem, with asserting that competition will help satisfy viewers' desires. This second difficulty stems from the fact that the spectrum is allocated by administrative fiat, not market prices. Consequently, we cannot know that the spectrum is being, or will be, devoted to the uses most highly valued by viewers. If the spectrum is "imperfectly" allocated in that sense, it is theoretically possible that monopoly rather than competition will come closer to satisfying viewers' desires "perfectly." Two wrongs do not make a right, but, given one wrong, another wrong can make the lesser evil. Nevertheless, for all the reasons expressed in the text, betting on competition seems preferable to betting on monopoly.

11. See, e.g., Red Lion Broadcasting Co. v. FCC, 395 U.S. 367 (1969); Mt. Mansfield Television, Inc. v. FCC, 442 F. 2d 470 (2d. Cir. 1971).

12. See D. H. Ginsburg, *Regulation of Broadcasting* (St. Paul: West Pub. Co., 1979), pp. 317–30.

13. See, e.g., Policy Statement on Comparative Broadcast Hearings, 1 FCC 2d 393, 397 (1965); Report and Statement of Policy Re: Commission En Banc Programming Inquiry, 20 RR 1901 (1960).

14. See, e.g., Policy Statement on Comparative Broadcast Hearings, 1 FCC 2d 393, 395–96 (1965).

15. See, e.g., N. Johnson, Broadcasting in America, 42 FCC 2d 3, 30–33 (1973).

16. See, e.g., Sixth Report and Order, 41 FCC 148, 167, 171–72 (1952) (allocation of television stations).

Chapter 4

1. The existing television regulations discussed in this chapter are codified at 47 C.F.R. § 73.658 (1983). A full description of their evolution appears in *New Networks 1*:445–62. To avoid excessive intrusion of lengthy citations, we have deliberately omitted replicating the detailed references to all the materials supporting the assertions in this text. Interested readers are referred instead to the aforementioned sources.

2. 11 Fed. Reg. 33 (1946).

3. *New Networks 2*:65–104.

4. 47 U.S.C. § 153(p) (1976).

5. T. G. Krattenmaker and A. R. Metzger, "FCC Regulatory Authority over Commercial Television Networks: The Role of Ancillary Jurisdiction," *Northwestern University Law Review* 77 (1982):403.

6. See L.A. Powe, "FCC Determinations on Networking Issues in Multiple Ownership Proceedings" 95–97, in FCC, Network Inquiry Special Staff: *Preliminary Report on Prospects for Additional Networks* (Feb. 1980).

7. Report, Statement of Policy and Order, 63 FCC 2d 674 (1977).

8. *Federal Register*, vol. 42, no. 17, pp. 4992–96 (Jan. 26, 1977).

9. A complete description of these consent decrees appears in *New Networks 2*: 653–716.

10. *New Networks 2*:201–7.

11. An extensive analysis of the structure and terms of these contracts, based upon review of the contract files of forty-seven network programs, appears in *New Networks 2*:445–95.

12. See the sources cited in nn. 8 and 9 above.

Chapter 5

1. The relationship could, in principle, involve the sale of all advertising time by the network with the entire receipts of stations coming in the form of payments from the network. Alternatively, all advertising time could be sold by stations with the network being compensated for programs through payments from stations. The method chosen will depend, in large measure, on the relative value of network and station advertising.

2. For 1980, revenues from the sale of station time to the major networks by their affiliates were about $310 million, while total broadcast revenues of affiliates were about $4.2 billion. FCC, *Television Broadcast Financial Data—1980*.

3. For 1980, broadcast profits for all affiliates was about $960 million while network profits were about $325 million (ibid.). Eliminating compensation would

have increased network profits to about $635 million, while reducing affiliation profits to about $650 million.

4. For a detailed description of affiliation contracts and their historical evolution, see *New Networks* 2:131–91.

5. The analysis presented here follows the general lines of the approach taken in S. M. Besen and R. Soligo, "The Economics of the Network-Affiliate Relationship in the Television Broadcasting Industry," *American Economic Review* 63 (1973):259–68. See also D. A. Graham and J. M. Vernon, "The Economics of the Network-Affiliate Relationship: Comment," *American Economic Review* 65 (1975):1032–36; S. M. Besen and R. Soligo, "The Economics of the Network-Affiliate Relationship: Reply," *American Economic Review* 65 (1975):1037–38.

6. See *New Networks* 2:270–73, 275–82 for an empirical analysis of station compensation.

7. Recall that the NBC affiliation agreement contains a "waived hour" provision rather than a deduction, but the effect is the same.

8. See *New Networks* 2:158–61.

9. Note that one effect of the ban on network representation of affiliates in the national spot market is to reduce the information available to networks about the value of their programs to affiliates.

10. For a discussion of the use of strategic behavior, see O. E. Williamson, *Markets and Hierarchies: Analysis and Antitrust Implications* (New York: The Free Press, 1975), chap. 2.

11. In practice, special compensation arrangements are usually made for sports programs.

12. For an empirical analysis of clearance behavior, see *New Networks* 2:273–75, 282–86.

13. Of course the rule has no effect on the behavior of stations owned by the network.

14. Under certain circumstances, such FCC policies may not lead to reduced clearance levels. For example, consider an affiliate such as the one depicted in table 5.2, but assume that there exists in its market an independent station that is an alternative affiliate for the network. Now, even if the station is offered only an amount just over 40 per program cleared, the affiliate may still clear A, B, and C, even though its reservation price for C is 50. This would occur if the affiliate feared that failure to clear all three programs might result in the transfer of its affiliation to the independent station. As long as the total amount of compensation paid leaves the station better off than if it were an independent, the station may be reluctant to threaten its affiliation, even though this may require it to clear programs for which the compensation paid is smaller than its reservation price. In fact, we observe higher clearance rates in markets where there are potential alternative affiliates than in markets where there are none, despite the fact that stations in these markets receive lower network compensation. See *New Networks* 2:284–86.

15. If no such effect occurred, the prohibition on graduated compensation plans could be made completely ineffective through the use of variations in advertising time. But since this is unlikely, changes in the mix of advertising minutes will be only an imperfect device for evading the restriction on compensation plans. It is impossible to determine, solely on *a priori* grounds, how large this offset will be.

Chapter 6

1. Of course, the "new" network could be more efficient than the displaced network.

2. We are assuming here that the network acquires ownership of these stations through Commission application procedures. If all or many stations are initially owned by nonnetwork entities, the analysis would be very similar to that where networks must affiliate with stations rather than own them.

3. Perhaps NBC's Blue radio network—which broadcast only "sustaining" programs—was designed for this purpose. Alternatively, the "excess" stations could simply duplicate the programming of the "first" affiliates in the market, but this tactic may also lead to governmental intervention.

4. This assumes that both existing networks and independent station owners have the same information regarding the prospects of new network entry. If networks have better information, they could pay something less than this amount.

5. If in fact NBC's Blue radio network was designed to deter new network entry, NBC seems to have borne the costs of such a strategy alone. But dual networking can be used for other purposes as well. Under our assumed environment, every incumbent network may have an incentive to establish a bonafide dual network: while total industry profits will fall, the profits of the network that programs two sets of affiliates may rise.

6. There is at least one other strategy the networks could adopt to forestall the loss of profit from new network entry. Instead of contracting with either existing or potential affiliates to prevent them from accepting the programs of new networks, the incumbents could buy the programs of the new networks. The price the incumbents would have to pay would be at least the profits the new network could have earned and may also include a share of the additional profits the incumbents earn from deterring entry. There is an additional problem with this approach: there may be a deluge of "potential networks," requiring the existing networks to distinguish between credible and "incredible" potential network entrants. Mere possession of a popular program may not be very good evidence that the self-described entrant is in fact a credible entrant. To put this in other terms, potential networks have made no irreversible investment in networking that would signal their intentions. Potential affiliates, on the other hand, have presumably made an investment that makes their threat to affiliate with new networks credible: they have invested in broadcast stations.

7. See chap. 2. See also R. E. Park, "New Television Networks" (Santa Monica:

The Rand Corporation, 1973) for an analysis based on 1971 data, and R. E. Park, "New Television Networks: An Update," *New Networks 1*:143–84, for an analysis based on 1978 data.

8. Report, Statement of Policy and Order, 63 FCC 2d 674, 679–80 (1977).

9. At the end of 1981, the most recent year for which data are available, of the 3,975 cable systems taking at least one pay service, 1,545 (39 percent) provided more than one service; P. Kagan Associates, *The Pay TV Newsletter* (December 31, 1981), p. 4.

10. Such policies may be desirable for noneconomic reasons as well. A policy that limits the number of channels that can be controlled by a single programmer may be supportable on "diversity of sources" grounds. For an analysis from an exclusively economic point of view, see S. M. Besen and L. L. Johnson, *An Economic Analysis of Mandatory Leased Channel Access to Cable Television* (Santa Monica: The Rand Corporation, 1982).

11. It is theoretically possible that the profits earned by adopting a mixed or totally unconventional affiliation pattern under the rule would be greater than profits earned by using conventional affiliates in absence of the rules. In these circumstances, the existence of the rules would not increase barriers to entry.

12. FCC, *Report on Chain Broadcasting*, 1941, Commission Order no. 37; docket 5060, May 1941, pp. 73–74.

13. G. M. Fournier and D. L. Martin, "Does Government-Restricted Entry Produce Market Power?: New Evidence from the Market for Television Advertising," *Bell Journal of Economics* 14 (1983):44.

14. However, the harm done to "competition" by such a policy may be minor. The very appearance of a new network catering to specialized audiences and advertisers indicates that these specialized advertisers now have another choice of medium on which to place their ads. Although differences in the nature of broadcasting compared to other media may impart a degree of monopoly power to the network, the birth of that network has the effect of increasing competition within the "media market" broadly defined.

15. If the preempted network program is the least popular (profitable) program in the market, it will not be shown in any event. For purposes of this discussion, we assume that the most popular programs are the most profitable programs.

16. This is the condition required for an affiliate to find it profitable to preempt the network program *and* for a network not to find it profitable to increase compensation payments to the affiliate to induce clearance of the network program. For the purposes of this discussion, we ignore preemptions by an affiliate that are designed solely to increase the network's compensation payments to it.

17. *New Networks 2*:263.

18. See 28 FCC 2d 169, 190–91 (1971).

19. FCC, Notice of Inquiry into Commercial Television Network Practices, 62 FCC 2d 548 (1977).

20. As of the end of 1983, there were approximately sixty networks supplying video, audio, and text programming to cable systems, including both advertiser- and

subscriber-supported services. See National Cable Television Ass'n, "Satellite Services Report" (March 1984).

21. Indeed, we should not be surprised if many of the new networks adopt compensation practices similar to those of the dominant, conventional networks.

22. In 1977, ABC, CBS, and NBC reported they were prefeeding eight and one-half to thirty hours per week of programming to their affiliates. See *New Networks* 2:204–5.

23. This principle is elaborated in chap. 9.

Chapter 7

1. *New Networks* 2:327–39.

2. Ibid., 347–72.

3. Ibid., 554–62.

4. In what follows we shall often refer to payments to program suppliers instead of using the more cumbersome phrase "payments to the factors of production that produce programs." It should be emphasized, however, that many of the payments by the networks to suppliers are simply "passed through" to talent and other programming inputs.

5. *New Networks* 2:554–62.

6. The analysis of this section, although couched in terms of syndication rights, would apply to any rights other than those to the initial network run. These include rights to foreign distribution, merchandising, and network daytime and late-night stripping.

7. Previously published analyses of the effects of the syndication rule are reviewed in *New Networks* 2: 531–39.

8. As explained below, this could occur even in the absence of a ban on network acquisition of syndication rights if, for some reason, the parties agreed to share the risk of program failure.

9. A description of present option contract practices appears in *New Networks* 2:467–69.

10. A description of spin-off protections obtained by networks appears in *New Networks* 2:473–75.

11. For a discussion of these alleged antitrust violations, see *New Networks* 2:657–77.

12. For example, a program entering its first season has a probability of .3 of returning the next season. See *New Networks* 2:427.

13. The precise distribution of expected profits in this case would depend on the same factors that affect the distribution of profits when there is no uncertainty. As noted above, the primary factor is the extent of competition among networks for programs.

14. Note that if the supplier is also risk-averse it may be no better off than before, even though its expected return has increased, because the risk it bears has risen also.

15. Even if four programs fail, the package of programs will show a profit since the

one profitable program earns 50 while each of the four failures loses only 10. The calculation of the probability that all five programs will fail is based on the assumption that the probability that any one program will succeed is independent of the probability that any other will succeed.

16. An audit of the supplier's books, however, would show the expenditure as 50. The extra resources could be employed, for example, on another project.

17. See the discussion in *New Networks* 2:357–58, 362–63.

18. Note that there is no inconsistency between suppliers receiving larger payments on average and their being made worse off, since the additional payments are accompanied by the need to bear larger risks. Of course, program suppliers will attempt to shift the risk, either among themselves or to other entities, such as independent syndicators.

19. If the network pays the supplier only its opportunity cost (including a risk premium), the supplier will be no better off and the network will be worse off.

20. That there has been some tendency toward increasing concentration in program supply since the rules' enactment is discussed in *New Networks* 2:556.

21. See Reply Comments of the Bureaus of Consumer Protection, Economics, and Competition of the Federal Trade Commission, BC Docket No. 82-345, Federal Communications Commission, pp. 42–43.

22. It should be noted that the extent of renegotiation of the network-supplier contract strongly suggests that suppliers do share in these unexpected revenues. See *New Networks* 2:488–94. For statistical evidence on this sharing, see J. R. Woodbury, S. M. Besen, and G. M. Fournier, "Determinants of Network Television Program Prices: Implicit Contracts, Regulation, and Bargaining Power," *Bell Journal of Economics* 14 (1983):351.

23. The role of the network in the program development and production process is described in *New Networks* 2:347–72.

24. This is, of course, the theory upon which copyright and patent laws are based.

25. This supply restriction is a consequence of the monopoly power conferred on the supplier—and temporarily ceded to the network—by virtue of its copyright on the program.

26. Cases may arise in which the sale of nonexclusive rights increases profits. For example, during its last network years, "M*A*S*H" was available on CBS and in syndication. Alternatively, networks might acquire exclusivity even for a program beyond its fifth season.

27. See the discussion in *New Networks* 2:473–74.

28. Ibid., 467–68.

Chapter 8

1. *New Networks* 2:327–47.

2. Declaratory Ruling on Section 73.658(j) (1) (ii), 88 FCC 2d 30 (1981).

3. Christian Broadcasting Network, Inc., FCC 81–471 (released October 9, 1981).

4. Notice of Proposed Rulemaking, 47 Fed. Reg. 32959 (1982); Tentative Decision and Request for Further Comments, BC Docket No. 82–345 (Aug. 12, 1983). At the request of several senators, and in the face of opposition to repeal voiced by President Reagan, the FCC agreed to postpone acting on the matter. See *Broadcasting* 38 (April 23, 1984).

5. 23 FCC 2d 382, 392–99.

6. See Mt. Mansfield Television v. FCC, 442 F.2d 470 (2d Cir. 1971).

7. See the discussion of the impact of PTAR on syndicated program production in *New Networks* 2:567–68.

8. 23 FCC 2d at 398, 399.

9. However, there is evidence that prior to the rules' enactment, the networks paid suppliers the full expected value of the syndication rights. See R.W. Crandall, "FCC Regulation, Monopsony and Network Television Program Cost," *Bell Journal of Economics and Management Science* 3 (1972):483–508.

10. See e.g., R.W. Crandall, "The Economic Effect of Television-Network Program Ownership," *Journal of Law and Economics* 14 (1971):405–6; T. L. Schuessler, "FCC Regulation of the Network Television Program Procurement Process: An Attempt to Regulate the Laws of Economics," *Northwestern Law Review* 73 (1978):301–2.

11. Crandall, "Economic Effect," pp. 405–6.

12. The two other less likely assumptions are that both the network and supplier are indifferent to risk or that one party is indifferent and the other is averse. If both are indifferent, the increased risk assumed by the supplier under the rules is not a matter of concern to either party. Any distribution of risk is efficient. If the supplier is indifferent to risk and the network is not, the supplier would assume all the risk whatever the rule. If the supplier is risk-averse, however, and the network is not, the rules have a perverse effect, because they prevent the network from bearing the risk that it otherwise would assume.

13. See *New Networks* 2:556.

14. The rules may inadvertently have increased the amount of locally produced programs by reducing the attractiveness of producing network programs.

15. MPAA et al., "Petition for Declaratory Ruling," FCC Docket 21049 (June 1, 1977).

16. A discussion of the extent of renegotiation can be found in *New Networks* 2:480–93. Statistical evidence is provided by J. R. Woodbury, S. M. Besen, and G.M. Fournier, "Determinants of Network Television Program Prices: Implicit Contracts, Regulation, and Bargaining Power," *Bell Journal of Economics* 14 (1983):351.

17. For a discussion of the bases for these suits, see *New Networks* 2:657–70.

18. See table F-24, appendix F, appendixes to FCC, Network Inquiry Special Staff: *An Analysis of Television Program Production, Acquisition and Distribution* (June 1980); FCC docket 21049.

19. On Sundays the networks have often utilized the exemptions for children's and public affairs' programs to broadcast a full prime-time schedule.

20. FCC, Network Inquiry Special Staff: *A Review of the Proceedings of the FCC Leading to the Adoption of the Prime Time Access Rule, the Financial Interest Rule, and the Syndication Rule,* p. 42 (October 1979).

21. See *New Networks* 2:738–39.

22. Ibid., 563–68.

23. See n. 3 above.

Chapter 9

1. See 47 U.S.C. § 201 et seq.; see also Computer and Communications Industry Ass'n v. FCC, no. 80–1471, slip op. at 25–26 (D.C. Cir. 1982); National Association of Regulatory Utility Comm'rs v. FCC, 525 F. 2d 630, 640–41 (D.C. Cir. 1976).

2. 47 C.F.R. § 73.636(a)(2) (1982). On the status of efforts to repeal this rule, see *Broadcasting* 82 (April 2, 1984).

3. 47 C.F.R. § 73.636(a)(1) (1982).

4. 47 C.F.R. § 73.501(a)(1) (1982). In 1981, the Commission granted CBS's request for a limited waiver of this restriction, allowing it to acquire cable systems so long as the aggregate number of subscribers at any time does not exceed one-half of one percent of the total number of U.S. cable subscribers or 40,000 subscribers, whichever is less. See Memorandum Opinion and Order, 87 FCC 2d 587 (1981).

5. Notice of Proposed Rulemaking, 47 Fed. Reg. 39,212 (1982).

6. Memorandum Opinion and Order, 87 FCC 2d 30 (1981), petition for stay denied, 87 FCC 2d 455 (1981).

7. United States v. ABC, 1981-1 Trade Cas. (CCH) ¶ 64,150 (C.D. Cal. 1980) (ABC decree); United States v. CBS, 1980-1 Trade Cas. (CCH) ¶ 63,594 (C.D. Cal. 1980) (CBS decree); United States v. NBC, 1978-1 Trade Cas. (CCH) ¶ 61,855 (C.D. Cal. 1977) (NBC decree).

8. 47 C.F.R. § 73.658(g) (1982).

9. Report and Order, 63 FCC 2d 674 (1977).

10. The so-called Charlotte Rule currently bars a network from acquiring a station "in any locality where the existing television broadcast stations are so few or of such unequal desirability (in terms of coverage, power, frequency or other related matters) that competition would be substantially restrained by such licensing"; 47 C.F.R. § 73.658 (f) (1982). Although the rule was intended to preclude a network from dominating a small market by acquiring a powerful station, in practice it has never prevented a network's acquisition of a local outlet. See L.A. Powe, "FCC Determinations on Networking Issues in Multiple Ownership Proceedings," in FCC, Network Inquiry Special Staff: *Prospects for Additional Networks* (Feb. 1980). In a series of cases in the 1950s, the Commission consistently held that the rule was inapplicable principally on the grounds that the markets in question had enough desirable stations to allay concerns about dominance. See, e.g., National Broadcast-

ing Co., 44 FCC 2098 (1960); St. Louis Telecast, Inc., 22 FCC 625 (1956). This experience suggests that the rule addresses a problem that is unlikely to occur: network acquisition of a station in a small market. Because the FCC limits any entity to ownership of five VHF (seven total) stations, networks are unlikely to seek licenses in small markets.

11. Second Report and Order, 23 FCC 2d 816 (1970).

12. Notice of Proposed Rulemaking, 47 Fed. Reg. 39, 212 (1982).

13. FCC, Office of Plans and Policy, *FCC Policy on Cable Ownership* (1981), p. 91.

14. See *Broadcasting* (Nov. 15, 1982), p. 52.

Chapter 10

1. See chap. 2.

2. See chap. 3.

3. See chap. 2.

4. See chap. 9.

5. See chaps. 7, 8 and 9.

6. See chaps. 5 and 6.

7. See chap. 9.

8. As explained in chap. 6, the existing prohibitions on networks' control of affiliates' advertising rates and on affiliates' acquisition of territorial exclusivity in network programs appear to serve the public interest in competition and diversity.

9. See chaps. 2 and 4.

10. For a detailed description of these events, see T. L. Schuessler, "The Effect of the FCC's Spectrum Management Policies upon the Number of Television Networks," in FCC, Network Inquiry Special Staff: *Preliminary Report on Prospects for Additional Networks* (Feb. 1980).

11. See chap. 2.

12. For a brief history of FCC regulation of long-distance telephone service, see S. M. Besen and J. R. Woodbury, "Regulation, Deregulation, and Antitrust in the Telecommunications Industry," *The Antitrust Bulletin* 28 (1983):44–47.

13. For a history of regulation in the airline industry, see G.W. Douglas and J. C. Miller, *Economic Regulation of Domestic Air Transport: Theory and Policy* (Washington, D.C.: Brookings Institution, 1974).

14. For a brief history of ICC regulation, see T. G. Moore, "The Beneficiaries of Trucking Regulation," *Journal of Law and Economics* 21 (1978):327.

15. See G. J. Stigler, "The Theory of Economic Regulation," *Bell Journal of Economics and Management Science* 2 (1971):3; S. Peltzman, "Toward a More General Theory of Regulation," *Journal of Law and Economics* 19 (1976):211.

16. Not all policies pursued by the FCC could have been intended to harm the networks. For example, the general restrictions on cable television growth undoubtedly benefited the networks as well as their affiliates. On the issue of cable

development, however, the FCC probably could not have helped the affiliates without also aiding the networks.

17. See chap. 2.

18. Home Box Office v. FCC, 567 F.2d 9 (D.C. Cir. 1977), cert. denied, 434 U.S. 829 (1977).

Index

ABC, 1–2; network rate of, 52; and territorial exclusivity rule, 44. *See also* Networks

Adjacencies: alteration in amount of, 53, 64; definition of, 51; network control of, 79–80; and net revenue of station affiliate, 53–55; of UHF stations, increase in value of, 86. *See also* Advertising time

Advertisers: advantages of networking to, 4–5, 6; demand level of, and number of networks, 8–9, 15; network acquisition of, 148; networks as intermediaries between audience and, 115–16; welfare of, and regulation, 24

Advertising time. *See also* Adjacencies; Promotional free-riding

—alteration in mix of, 64, 170

—network-affiliate division of, 50–51

—revenues from sale of, in multiple-station exhibition of programs, 120

—sale of, rule against network representation in: arguments for, and evaluation of, 67, 79–83; statement of, 35

—station rates for, rule against network control of: arguments for, and evaluation of, 67, 79–82; repeal of, in radio broadcasting, 44; statement of, 35

—value of: and new network entry, 72; and Prime Time Access Rule, 141

Affiliates. *See* Network affiliates

Affiliation contract. *See* Exclusive affiliation rule; Network-affiliate relationship, economic analysis of; Term of affiliation rule

American Telephone and Telegraph Company (AT&T), 10, 148, 174

Ancillary jurisdiction, 13, 23

Antisiphoning rules, 11–12, 16, 19

Antitrust law: application of, to networks, 166, 169; and competition, 25; and market power acquisition, 152. *See also* Department of Justice, antitrust suits of; Sherman Antitrust Act

Audience-flow effects, 120

Bargaining power: of network affiliates, 57; of producers, 130–35. *See also* Strategic bargaining

Barrow Report, 32, 33, 35